'EFFEC

On-the-Job

TRAINING,

Developing Library Human Resources

Sheila D. Creth

AMERICAN LIBRARY ASSOCIATION
Chicago and London 1986

Designed by Charles Bozett

Composed by Precision Typographers, Inc.,
in Baskerville. Display type,
Gillies Light, composed by
Pearson Typographers

Printed on 50-pound Glatfelter,
a pH-neutral stock, and bound in
10-point Carolina cover stock by
Edwards Brothers, Inc.

Library of Congress Cataloging-in-Publication Data

Creth, Sheila D.
Effective on-the-job training.

1. Library employees—In-service training.
2. Librarians—In-service training. 3. Library education
(Continuing education) 4. Library personnel management.
I. Title.
Z668.5.C73 1986   023′.8   86–14187
ISBN 0–8389–0441–6

CONTENTS

PREFACE   v

1.   OVERVIEW OF THE TRAINING PROCESS   1
       Critical Role of Training   1
       Objectives of Training   3
       Process and Attitude   3
       The Corporate Culture and Socialization   4
       Change Agent   5
       Staff Resistance   7
           Exercise   8
       Role of the Supervisor   9
       Factors Contributing to Inadequate Training   10
       False Assumptions about Training   12
           Exercise   14
       Learning Principles   14
       Adult Learning Environment   15
           Exercise   16

2.   SPECIFIC TRAINING NEEDS   17
       New Employee   17
       Performance Improvement   20
       Operational Problems or Changes   22
           Exercise   25

3.   PLANNING FOR TRAINING   26
       Job Analysis   27
           Example   30
           Exercise   32
       Performance Standards   32

Example   35
Exercise   36
Training Objectives   36
Example   37
Examples   38
Exercise   38
Sequence for Training   39
Exercise   41
Selecting and Training Trainers   41
Exercise   43
Training Methods   43
Exercise   49
Writing the Training Plan   49
Exercise   51

4.   IMPLEMENTATION OF TRAINING   53
Motivation   53
Aspects of Training Requiring Special Attention   58
Exercise   66
Materials   67
Exercise   70
Scheduling Training   70
Exercise   72

5.   EVALUATION OF TRAINING   73
Who Evaluates   75
What to Evaluate   76
When and How to Evaluate   79
Analyzing Evaluation Information   83
Exercise   84

6.   BEYOND THE TRAINING PLAN   85
Coaching and Role Modeling   86
Goal Setting   87
Other Training Sources   88
Training in the Electronic Library   91
Summary   96

Appendix A   JOB TRAINING PLANS   97
Clerical Positions   97
Technical Positions   104
Professional Positions   110

Appendix B   ORIENTATION CHECKLIST   117

INDEX   119

PREFACE

After more than a decade in library personnel administration, I have come to believe that improved job training is an unrealized source for library effectiveness. As I talked with supervisors, and to staff, regarding a seemingly infinite number of work problems (performance, communication, attitude, morale, etc.), I began to realize that a number of barriers that were preventing acceptable performance and contributing to poor work relationships appeared to develop during job training.

Too often, I encountered situations in which enthusiastic and energetic library job applicants became apathetic or disillusioned employees within a few months; clearly something had occurred in the interim. Exit interviews with staff also disclosed an all-too-familiar picture of neglect during job training both for new staff and staff who were faced with learning new assignments, procedures, or equipment. Indeed, most staff did acquire the required skills and knowledge, though not necessarily in either an efficient or effective manner. But the more damaging consequence of poor job training was the attitude that library staff were likely to project about their work, their supervisors, the library as an organization, and even their value as people in the organization.

During this time, while I was involved in creating staff development programs with particular focus on supervisory training, I became convinced that departmental job training, while a crucial link, was not getting the attention it needed. Therefore, I began to focus more on the process of job training—what was happening and how it could be improved—and eventually developed a workshop on the job training process.

The response to this workshop over the past six years has demonstrated that supervisors are eager to improve or enhance job training.

This book has grown out of the materials and ideas originally developed for the workshop and has been written to be an aid to supervisors. For this reason, there are exercises throughout the book that should be helpful to supervisors and trainers as they begin to consider other facets of job training. In addition, the Appendix contains samples of job training plans from other libraries that should assist readers in developing their own job training plans.

The purpose of the book is to suggest not only that there is a "better" way to conduct job training but also that it is possible to establish a better environment in which staff can learn and contribute. A "seat-of-the-pants" approach is used far too frequently to provide job training, with the result being that staff performance and morale land squarely on their derrière.

The process of job training described in this book is a demanding one in that it requires time, energy, and commitment from the supervisor. The results, though, will be rewarding for everyone involved. People seek to belong, to develop a commitment to their work and to their colleagues, and to take pride in their efforts. The book attempts to identify ways for supervisors to meet these needs. Knowledge and skills training built on this foundation will be far more effective.

There are a number of people—both those whom I have trained and those who have trained me—who have influenced the development of my own ideas and concepts about training. In addition, I have benefited from the ideas of the hundreds of people who have participated in the job training workshop that I have conducted in a number of libraries and at conferences.

I have also benefited from discussions with colleagues in the profession who are committed to and involved with staff development. In particular, my discussions over the past several years with Anne Lipow of the University of California at Berkeley and with Maureen Sullivan of Yale University have always produced a gem of an idea or a spark of excitement that I have been able to plow back into training and development.

In writing this book, I received invaluable assistance from Dottie Eakin of the University of Michigan as she read and commented on the early drafts of the manuscript. I was fortunate to have editorial assistance as well from Ann Dougherty, associate editor of the *Journal of Academic Librarianship*. The final result, while reflecting the contributions of colleagues and friends, is fully my responsibility.

Training is hard—damn hard—but the result is worth the effort; and what could be more satisfying than to contribute to another person's growth and learning?

1

OVERVIEW OF
THE TRAINING PROCESS

Critical Role of Training

No one would deny that learning is a necessary process for activities that we must perform and skills we must use throughout every aspect of our daily lives. Each day is filled with situations for which we must be educated, trained, and oriented in order to manage in our complex world. In these various situations, it is not sufficient to have knowledge; we also must acquire the skills that enable us to use the knowledge, gain confidence in our ability to make judgments, and ultimately feel secure in the environments in which we function.

Through daily experiences, we are also aware of the quality of training received by others. If we were to step back and think about our daily experiences, we would recognize and applaud the training that results in pleasant and efficient service. We would also criticize organizations for inadequate training, which results in poor service. In many situations, we take the training of others for granted and trust that adequate preparation has been provided by those in charge. For instance, when we board an airplane we assume that the pilot knows and understands the operation of the airplane and is knowledgeable about the route and all of the rules of the air in order to assure our safe arrival at the correct destination. We assume that the accountant preparing our tax return or the lawyer handling a legal case for us is knowledgeable about and adequately trained in current procedures and guidelines and can be effective in carrying out his or her responsibilities.

While the relationship between trained and competent staff and quality service is readily apparent to us in situations in which we are

1

the recipients of service, we are seldom as critically objective about the training—and thus the service—our own organizations provide. Too often, supervisors fail to realize that poor performance and poor service within their own department may result from inadequate training. Attention to job training is essential for a number of reasons that relate very specifically to the ability of libraries to maintain their vitality and central role in an increasingly complex and competitive information society.

Libraries as service organizations are affected by the satisfaction that patrons feel. The level of user satisfaction eventually translates into the level and quality of support that the library receives from the parent organization. Therefore, poor training can have a direct impact on the health of the organization. Even when strong support exists for a library, it is not likely that future budget increases will be allocated for the acquisition of additional staff. Indeed, with the expansion of technology there may be pressure to cut the library staff. Therefore, current or reduced staffing levels will have to be sufficient to respond to new and increased demands. This change in staffing will require more attention to training so that staff can handle more diverse and demanding assignments.

Libraries must also be flexible in meeting the changing requirements of the user population. Library staff will have to be able to assess the needs of the library community, predict directions, and identify new services as well as those that are no longer in demand. If the library staff waits until user dissatisfaction points to new needs or obsolete activities, the library will be seen as a passive, non-responsive organization. Thus, staff need to be prepared to respond effectively to the changing context of library and information services while maintaining respect for traditional values.

Finally, the widening scope and accelerated pace of technology within library and information services are placing new demands on library staff. Not only will library staff continue to see an increase in the use of automation in their work, but the technology itself will not remain stable. Thus, adaptation to different automated systems and types of technology will be necessary. The only factor in library organizations that may remain constant is change itself.

As a result of these changing circumstances, library staff will require an impressive array of knowledge, skills, and abilities in order to be effective. Supervisors therefore need to rethink their role in training, their approach to training, and the long-term impact that training has on the individual and on the library itself. The future of libraries relies on the quality, dedication, energy, and intelligence of the library staff. Training plays a central role in ensuring that staff are prepared.

Objectives of Training

The primary objective of job training is to bring about a change—an increase in knowledge, the acquisition of a skill, or the development of confidence and good judgment. Job training is not successful unless the person can do something new or different or demonstrate a change in behavior.

There are three dimensions in each job that an employee must master in order to perform effectively: knowledge, skill, and ability.

Knowledge refers to the information that is needed to perform a set of activities efficiently and effectively. Examples are knowledge of reference tools, cataloging practices, collection developments, automated circulation systems, call numbers, management topics, and many more.

Skill refers to the techniques, the approaches, and the styles of translating knowledge into action or practice. For instance, librarians need the skill to conduct a reference interview, to interpret cataloging rules in relation to the intellectual content of the material, and to evaluate staff performance.

Ability refers to the intangible qualities or characteristics that are necessary for performance and are often referred to under the rubric of "motivation" or "attitude." Abilities needed by library staff include flexibility, cooperation, service attitude, and leadership.

Job training should be structured to consist of both formal and informal activities that address each of these three dimensions—knowledge, skill, and ability—and the goals of training should be clear enough so that the trainee understands what outcome or behavior is desired. Ignoring any one of the three components will create an impact on job performance at some time during the person's employment. Typically, job training has focused narrowly on providing instruction in specific information, procedures, or equipment required in the performance of job tasks. While these aspects of training will always be essential, the results will be inadequate to meet library needs if a broader context is not provided and if the needs of the individual employee are ignored.

Process and Attitude

A dramatic improvement in the results achieved from job training can be realized if attention is given to the *process* of training. Questions to ask oneself include what is happening to the person being trained, what are the person's feelings, and what needs does the person have as new tasks or an entire new job assignment is being learned? During the training process more is happening to the trainee than his or her simply learning a skill; indeed, the trainee is developing an *attitude* about the job, the supervisor, co-workers, and the library. It is this attitude that will have the most effect on the person's future success in his or her immediate assignment and in any other jobs assumed during a library career.

Too often, it is during the training period that a staff member develops a poor attitude because of the manner in which he or she is treated at this critical time. As most supervisors already know, it is possible to retain someone who has not grasped particular information or become as skillful in a task performance as required, but trying to alter someone's attitude is virtually impossible. A major barrier to altering a person's attitude is that attitude cannot be observed or measured; only behavior can be observed. A supervisor may assume that an employee has a "poor attitude," but it remains an assumption only. In addition, people hold onto feelings and beliefs more tenaciously than they do to the manner in which they perform routines or procedures. This fact also presents a substantial difficulty in attempting to alter a perceived poor attitude held by an employee. While there are mechanisms for trying to address such a situation, attitude change requires skill and tact and is a long-term process. The main objective of training, therefore, should be to create an environment in which positive attitudes will develop initially.

The Corporate Culture and Socialization

In developing a new concept of the training process, supervisors and trainers need to acknowledge and understand the *corporate culture* that operates within their library. All organizations are social settings with specific requirements for behavior, communication, roles and responsibilities, and rewards and punishments. Drake characterizes the corporate culture as representing a "set of values and beliefs shared by people working in an organization. It represents employees' collective judgments about the future based on past corporate rewards and punishments, heroes, villains, myths, successes and failures."[1] She goes on to

1. Miriam Drake, "Managing Innovation in Academic Libraries," *College and Research Libraries* 40 (Nov. 1979):504.

say that "understanding the corporate culture and acting in accordance with the culture often determines a person's success or failure on the job. A qualified and competent employee may fail because he or she doesn't fit in, while a less competent person who understands the culture has a higher probability of success."

An important aspect of training, then, is for the person to learn and adapt to the corporate culture. This process, referred to as *socialization*, encompasses how each of us learns how to behave in a particular environment, what the values and philosophy are of the people and the organization, what formal and informal guidelines exist for acceptable behavior, what the rewards and punishments are for behavior, and what the accepted roles and relationships are among members of the organization. Socialization is the process by which we learn about the world around us without having a rule book; instead we learn by listening, watching, and absorbing. The process of socialization occurs whenever we enter a new social setting. The quality of this process of integrating people into the library organization will determine largely whether they succeed or fail.

This understanding of the corporate culture and the socialization process is particularly critical when change is introduced into the library. Depending on the magnitude of the change (such as the expansion of automation), there may be serious disruption to the existing culture, making implementation difficult. In such situations, library administrators and supervisors need to identify the characteristics of the library's culture and determine where those characteristics are not consistent with long-range objectives. Education and training can then be used to adjust and strengthen the desired culture needed to support the new environment.

Change Agent

First and foremost, training should be seen as a *change agent*. As already indicated, training should result in some change in behavior, i.e., the demonstration of knowledge or of a skill not previously held. Equally important is that through training, the supervisor can prepare the person to operate successfully in the library environment over a long period of time. Supervisors must focus on their responsibility to prepare staff for potential long-term employment. Given this view of training, the supervisor's responsibility assumes a library-wide emphasis not just a departmental one. Typically, supervisors take a short-term view of training, particularly for clerical positions where turnover may be highest. Supervisors, thinking that a minimal commitment has been made, thus make a minimal investment in the person. Often, though, the employee moves to another position in the library, and the initial job training, including the attitudes already formed, will move with that employee. If job training does not address the need to build self-confidence, loyalty, respect for others, and a host of other positive attitudes, then the employee has been only partially trained. The knowledge and skills the person possesses may be sound, but the individual's overall ability to contribute and to adapt to future changes will be lacking.

The supervisor can also use the training process to begin to make a shift or change in the existing culture. For instance, if the supervisor desires more cooperation or improved communication, the training of a new employee (or training of all staff for a new system) is one of the ways to begin articulating these values and desired behaviors. As the view of training is expanded to include these other, more subtle components, attention should be given to the individual who will perform the job rather than focused solely on training the individual for job tasks. This shift in training perspective will allow recognition of the trainee's need to understand the ''mores'' of the work environment.

Finally, job training should reflect the reality of the library organization as a place in which change is constant. As staff are trained in specific knowledge and skills, the supervisor also needs to build in a recognition that change will occur in the work and that the ability of employees to change is valued and expected. Libraries are full of valuable and valued traditions, but many of these are being challenged and altered; staff are often not prepared to let go of old ways and thus to accept new approaches or requirements. It is through the training process that supervisors can assist staff in cultivating an attitude that will enable them to work effectively within the constantly changing environment. This process is a challenge, since training typically focuses on building a commitment to the task at hand, learning it, and carrying it out in a defined way. In the future, individuals will need to develop a dual attitude toward their work; they will need to have commitment and respect for the way work is currently performed combined with a willingness to alter and to let go of current practices when change is required. Training of a reference librarian is an example. The primary focus of training would be to ensure that the librarian has a commitment to the value of reference service, the ability to provide instruction in current services and activities, and the flexibility to respond to changes in the future. Unless training addresses this range of needs, the reference librarians will be wedded to the idea that reference service can be provided only at the reference desk using traditional tools, and he or she would potentially lack the flexibility to rethink reference service in the context of new technologies or changing user needs.

Staff Resistance

Staff resistance to change is a topic often heard discussed by supervisors when a new procedure or activity is to be implemented, particularly when automation is involved. Seldom, though, are complaints about staff resistance to change expressed as a problem of staff lacking the skill or ability to perform in the new environment. The concern is most often expressed by supervisors as an attitude problem, i.e., staff not being willing to accept the new system or procedure, or staff holding onto the old way, the old requirements. While there will occasionally be difficulties for some staff in adapting to a change because they lack certain knowledge or skills, the most prevalent problem is attitude.

There are legitimate reasons for resistance to change in the workplace. These fall into three broad categories: the fear of losing control, the fear of losing something of value, and an absence of personal benefit. Each of these concerns may come into play depending on the magnitude of the proposed change. For instance, in introducing automation, staff may fear that they will lose control because of the rigidity of the system requirements and because their work is hidden, kept out of sight, in the terminal. Some staff may feel that their work will be more closely monitored or that others will have access to information that only they knew about previously. Finally, staff may fear that automation will diminish their ability to exercise judgment and creativity in their work.

Fear of loss of control is very much related to a sense of losing something of value with the change, such as skills, recognition, status, or relationships. It is this social aspect of change that is often overlooked even though it is the dimension most likely to produce resistance. Malinconico states that "resistance is a distress signal from individuals that feel themselves impelled in a direction they find forbidding. The problem is not how to deal with resistance to change, but rather how to avoid it . . . ."[2]

Supervisors should recognize the legitimacy of staff concerns and identify ways to prevent resistance rather than assume that resistance always develops or that staff wish to be difficult. A valuable approach to preventing resistance is through job training, in which supervisors actively address the expectation that staff will be able to adapt to change, that they will recognize the need for change, and that they indeed will initiate change. Through the training process, supervisors can begin to build a staff that is flexible and resilient.

2. S. Michael Malinconico, "Technology, Change and People: Hearing the Resistance," *Library Journal* 108 (Jan. 15, 1983):112.

To achieve these broader objectives in training, supervisors must focus on the person being trained as well as the work to be performed. There is a need to be far more sensitive to the needs of the trainee, because by strengthening the training process the library, in turn, will be strengthened through its staff.

Exercise

This exercise is intended to assist supervisors and trainers in being more sensitive to the feelings and needs of employees in a learning environment. Specifically, it is meant to focus on the socialization that occurs during training and on the impact that positive and negative feelings which emerge during training have on the employee's long-term commitment and performance. The exercise can be done alone or with supervisor(s) and trainer(s) together.

1. Think about one of the first jobs you ever had in an organization, probably during high school or college. Think about how you felt during the first two to three weeks on the job. Make a column with the heading ''positive feelings'' and one with the heading ''negative feelings.'' Then list those feelings that you can recall—first the positive, then the negative.

2. Now review the lists that you have compiled and try to identify what occurred on the job that contributed first to your positive feelings and then to your negative feelings.

3. Once this review is completed, think of a position you assumed more recently, and repeat this process of writing down the feelings that you can recall and what job experiences might have contributed to those feelings.

4. Now compare both of these lists and see if you find similarities between the two sets of feelings. You probably will even though you were more mature and had greater experience in the latter situation.

5. Finally, review the lists of positive feelings and ask what is happening in your department during the training process that is likely to generate positive feelings. Next, review the lists of negative feelings and ask what may be happening in your department that could be contributing to negative feelings by staff.

Most often the feelings that people recall from the initial few weeks in a new job are negative ones such as anger, hostility, fear, stupidity or ignorance, and isolation. These negative feelings unfortunately are not easily shed as you have demonstrated with what you recall from your past experiences. They are also likely to influence a trainee's performance and commitment to the library. The positive feelings are the ones that should represent goals for job training.

Ask yourself the following questions as well to help focus on what may need improvement in your department's training:

What are the positive characteristics of the culture in your library and department? What are the negative characteristics?

What specific steps could you take to increase a new employee's motivation?

If better quality training had occurred in your department over the past year or so, what current problems would not exist or what new initiatives would have been possible?

What do you consider the greatest benefit that would come from improved training in your department?

Role of the Supervisor

Clearly, the person most influential in the training process is the supervisor who has the primary responsibility for developing staff. Supervisors' commitment to staff should include major attention to job training. Training, or learning, goes on even if supervisors ignore it or treat it in a cursory manner. Staff will train themselves by trial and error or by observing others. The process of learning by self-training frequently results in incorrect information and poor performance, particularly if the new employee learns from a poor or marginal performer. Also, the possibility of learning a job adequately through an informal process of observation or with a seat-of-the-pants approach is increasingly difficult in the more complicated automated environment of most libraries. In the past, it might have been feasible for a new staff member to bluff through a task for which he or she had been poorly trained. For instance, a poorly trained circulation clerk could improvise in processing a manual circulation transaction if uncertain about proper procedures but would be unable to do the same in using an online circulation system.

Therefore, the choice is not whether to train staff but how effective a supervisor wishes the training to be. Too often, supervisors assume that learning will just happen and that no specific plan of action or training schedule is required. Even when a supervisor recognizes the need to provide training, he or she too often focuses solely on the procedural or mechanical tasks to be performed, ignoring the background or "whys" of the operation. Also often overlooked is the need of the person being trained to understand, to receive encouragement, to be allowed to test his or her knowledge and skills in small increments, to learn from mistakes, and to receive feedback on progress. Training is oftentimes *ad hoc* in approach: as questions arise, they are answered; as problems occur, the employee is corrected or reprimanded. A systematic approach to training is often lacking, yet the benefits of a well-conceived and well-implemented training program so outweigh the time required to prepare and conduct one that the neglect of this activity is perplexing.

Factors Contributing to Inadequate Training

Several factors may contribute to inadequate training in libraries. First, the administration may place such a high priority on production and on having a "body at the desk" that the supervisor feels that little time beyond the bare minimum can be devoted to training. In addition, many libraries find themselves seriously understaffed and need to move quickly to put someone at a service desk even if he or she is poorly prepared. Second, the organization may place a high value on a trouble-shooting, problem-solving approach to management rather than on a preventive, planned approach. Thus, supervisors are discouraged from expending time and effort to develop training plans that may not be valued by the administrators. Third, there exists in the profession a view that a number of library tasks or jobs are dull and boring, or at best unattractive. Therefore, why devote much time to training for these jobs? While this is a view most often held about clerical tasks, occasionally it is displayed toward professional work as well. In any case, it is an attitude not likely to encourage a commitment to the work and thus to the training. Even with these limitations, supervisors must find effective ways of providing sound and comprehensive training. The costs to a library of a poorly trained staff are high, while the benefits of a well-trained staff are numerous (Table 1).

TABLE 1. *Costs vs. Benefits of Training*

Costs of Poor Training	Benefits from Sound Training
Poor performance	Increase in quality of work
Unacceptable productivity including high error rate	Increase in quantity of work
Increased supervision required	Reduced need for close and constant supervision, freeing supervisors for other activities
High turnover	Confident, flexible staff with low turnover
Discipline and motivational problems	High staff morale and job satisfaction

A supervisor has to be concerned with the costs of a poorly trained staff and conversely with the benefits of a staff who are knowledgeable and skilled as well as confident and flexible. The supervisor is the person in the organization who can most directly influence the environment that affects staff attitudes toward the job, toward co-workers, toward the library, and ultimately toward themselves as members of the library organization. The supervisor's active support of a well-planned, responsive training process will, in large part, contribute to whether an employee feels encouraged to participate in learning in an active way, develops self-confidence in his or her ability to succeed, and develops positive values toward the work and toward the importance of his or her contributions.

The supervisor's role in training and developing employees begins when they are first hired. The time and attention given by the supervisor to the planning of the initial job training for a new employee indicates the value that the supervisor places on a knowledgeable and able staff. This is also the opportunity to demonstrate support for the employee as the individual meets new people and learns new duties and surroundings. Supervisors should review the training that occurs in their departments to determine if the following conditions exist:

A strong sense of support for the person to succeed

A sense that the person has value to the organization because of the importance of the work and of the person

A recognition that the person has knowledge, skills, and abilities that are worthwhile to the library

An understanding that the success of the person will contribute to the department and to the library

A sense that as an individual, the person is a welcome addition to the staff.

Supervisors often complain—and with some justification—that they have too little influence on various aspects of employment such as the salary program, benefits, and personnel policies. Training, though, is an activity in which each supervisor can have a major impact and effect on the quality of the unit operations and on the individual employee's morale. In rethinking the training process and their own role, supervisors should see themselves as *teachers*. As a teacher, the supervisor provides information, direction, and guidance, and exercises a commitment to the overall development of staff. Supervisors should be enthusiastic about and excited by the possibility of contributing to another person's growth and development; there can be no more rewarding activity for a supervisor than the development of people.

Finally, supervisors need to recognize the dynamic and critical link between effective training and the attitudes that employees develop. It is these attitudes that will contribute most heavily to employees' success and to their ability to adapt to the changing environment.

Supervisors should review their own job responsibilities and priorities to ensure that they make the necessary commitment of time and energy to job training. Another important step is for supervisors and trainers to consider typical false assumptions that exist about the training activity and that will influence the quality of training.

False Assumptions about Training

When false assumptions about job training exist and are not recognized, difficulties during training are very likely to occur although they may not be immediately obvious. These false assumptions are often held by supervisors and trainers, and even occasionally by trainees, but they are seldom acknowledged. A number of false assumptions typically held include the following:

1. Training is simple.
2. Real training is informal.
3. Good employees train themselves.
4. Fast learners will be good employees; slow learners will be poor employees.
5. Trainees will always ask questions when they do not understand something.
6. Experienced staff do not need training.
7. There is only one right way to train.
8. Simple tasks are simple for everyone.
9. It is not good for the trainee if trainers indicate a lack of knowledge or a mistake.
10. Trainers can make someone learn.
11. Explaining once is enough.
12. Good materials will guarantee successful training.
13. Understanding will develop over time without explanation.
14. Review of the trainee's performance after the formal training is completed is not necessary.

What are the effects of some of these false assumptions on the training process? A review of the incorrect assumption that training is simple will provide a useful example. If a supervisor assumes that the process of learning a new job is simple and, therefore, that training someone is simple, then he or she is not motivated to invest much time in planning for and instructing the employee. In this type of situation, the training is not likely to be well thought out in terms of the content, the sequence for learning the knowledge and skills required, or the materials and equipment needed. The employee will arrive on the job to find that no one is quite sure what to do with him or her. Information about how to perform duties will be provided in bits and pieces, resulting in confusion and discouragement for the trainee.

The mistaken view that training is a simple activity usually results in wasted time spent in retraining, as well as in frustration for the supervisor and the employee, and possibly even for the public through poor service. In addition, the trainee might perceive that the supervisor feels that the work to be accomplished is not considered valuable enough to deserve careful and planned training or that the employee is not valued sufficiently to invest time in his or her training. In either case, this initial contact between the trainee and the job does not contribute to a positive basis for future interactions nor will it likely lead to desired results in performance.

Another false assumption that is often made by supervisors and trainers is that trainees will always ask questions when they do not understand something. This overlooks the fact that a trainee is in a vulnerable position; that is, he or she is new to the library, to the job, or to an automated system. No one wants to demonstrate ignorance. It is necessary for trainers to consider their training styles to be sure that they make it easy and comfortable for trainees to indicate a lack of knowledge or understanding. A question from a trainer such as ''Did you understand that?'' is not likely to get the result wanted. In fact, it is not unusual for the false assumption that trainees will ask questions to be coupled with the mistaken view that training and learning are simple. In this situation, the trainer will often make a remark such as ''Well, that was simple, but do you have any questions?'' This suggests to the trainee that only a simpleton would have a question, and thus only the most assertive and confident will speak up. In other situations, the trainer is so involved in explaining or demonstrating, that the trainee cannot find a point at which to interject a question.

If the trainer is not alert to non-verbal signals of confusion or distress, questions will surely go unanswered. Trainers therefore need to think about how they present information and whether they build into the training process opportunities for the trainee to ask questions, repeat information, and demonstrate skills. The trainer has to go beyond asking if the trainee has questions and create a comfortable environment for the trainee. This means that the trainee should know that a question will not result in a reprimand or even in a non-verbal signal that the question was unnecessary.

Any of these false assumptions will have a negative impact on the quality of training. Supervisors and trainers need to recognize that false assumptions and misconceptions about training do exist, identify them, and work to minimize their impact on the training process. In addition, supervisors need to recognize that certain principles apply to learning, and these principles should be considered when planning for training.

Exercise

This exercise can be performed alone or by a supervisor and trainer working together.

1. Review the false assumptions about training. Make a list of those that you hold about training.

2. Discuss the difficulties that may arise as a result of these assumptions. Try to be specific, using the examples provided in the text. Use your own experience as a trainer or trainee during your own career.

3. Discuss what corrections should be made in the training process to minimize or eliminate these false assumptions.

Learning Principles

In reassessing the training process, it is helpful to be familiar with principles that govern learning in any setting. Indeed, when these principles of learning are recognized, many of the false assumptions that are held about training and learning will be challenged. By recognizing that learning principles exist, the supervisor can be more realistic in setting expectations for training results and more sensitive to patterns of normal learning behavior. The following learning principles are particularly relevant to the training situation:

1. People learn when they are ready to learn.
2. Learning is an active not a passive function.
3. Learning occurs through trial and error.
4. Learning occurs through association.
5. Learning is multisensory.
6. People usually learn one thing at a time.

7. People must understand in order to learn.
8. Learning occurs from practice.
9. Positive feedback is necessary for learning.
10. Learning is unique to the individual.
11. Learning is affected by the order in which information is presented.
12. Rate of forgetting tends to be rapid immediately after learning.
13. Learning is increased if knowledge of results is understood.
14. Learning something new can interfere with remembering something learned earlier.

A review of these principles in relation to actual training practices and styles can assist supervisors and trainers in modifying the training process in order to achieve a more satisfactory result from the training activity.

Adult Learning Environment

Another aspect of job training that needs to be incorporated into efforts for improving training is a recognition of the special requirements for the adult learning environment. Knowles has identified a number of considerations that should be useful for supervisors and trainers as they consider departmental training:

> Treating mistakes as occasions for learning
> Helping trainees diagnose their own needs for self-improvement
> Involving participants in planning, carrying out, and evaluating their own training activities
> Making use of past experience of the trainee in the learning process
> Providing immediate opportunities to practice new learning.[3]

Knowles points out that adults need to be involved if learning is to be significant and lasting.[4] He goes on to say that adults see themselves as owners of unique experience that they wish to invest in learning, that they desire immediate application of what they have learned, and that they profit more from self-directed learning than from authoritarian learning situations. He suggests that it is important to distinguish effective learn-

3. Malcolm S. Knowles, *The Adult Learner: A Neglected Species*, 3rd ed. (Houston: Gulf Publishing, 1984).
4. Malcolm S. Knowles, *The Modern Practice of Adult Education: Androgogy versus Pedagogy* (New York: Association Pr., 1970), p.44.

ing situations for adults from those that are more appropriate for children.

Rogers has identified a number of similar considerations for adult learning, including the following: (1) people have a natural potential to learn; (2) significant learning occurs when the subject matter is relevant to the student's purpose; (3) learning that is perceived as self-threatening is resisted but less so if external controls are at a minimum; (5) significant learning is acquired through doing; (6) learning is facilitated when trainees participate responsibly in the process; (7) self-initiated learning that involves feelings as well as intellect is more lasting; (8) independence, creativity, and self-reliance are facilitated when self-evaluation and self-criticism are basic and evaluation by others is minimal or secondary; and (9) the most socially useful learning consists of learning the process of learning, developing a continuing openness to experience, and incorporating into oneself the process of change.[5]

Both Knowles and Rogers are suggesting that it is necessary to assess training activities to determine if they are likely to result in effective learning situations for adults.

In summary, much requires attention in the job training process if supervisors and libraries are to be successful through the efforts of their staff. While the remainder of the book places considerable emphasis on the need to be well organized in planning the specific steps in job training, the elements that relate to the individual trainee cannot be overlooked without the risk of failure in this important activity.

Exercise

This exercise can be conducted alone or with the supervisor and trainer together.

1. Review the previous sections on learning principles and the adult learning environment. Identify what conditions currently exist in your department that might ignore the learning principles or be in contrast to an effective adult learning environment.

2. Identify what changes could be implemented to improve job training in both of these areas.

---

5. Carl R. Rogers, *Freedom to Learn* (Columbus, Ohio: Merrill, 1969).

2

SPECIFIC TRAINING NEEDS

Although training should be viewed as a continuous process, not as a series of separate or unrelated incidents in a person's work life, there are situations, nonetheless, that require specific attention and an organized approach to learning for the employee. Though these training situations have a great deal in common, it is helpful for supervisors to recognize the distinct differences in their contexts and requirements. The situations are new employee, performance improvement, and operational problems or changes.

New Employee

What are the needs of the new employee, and how do they differ from the needs of other employees who need training? The most significant difference for the new employee is the obvious fact of being *new*. The new employee, in no matter what position or level of the organization and no matter how much previous work experience he or she has had, will initially experience a great deal of disorientation and anxiety. The new employee will be undergoing a learning process not only related to policies, procedures, and job duties, but he or she also will be learning about his or her role in the organization, the expected behaviors, the personalities and styles of other staff, and, more generally, the culture of the organization. During the initial period in a new job, the individual operates to a large extent in a vacuum regarding behavior and performance expectations, and lacks the full range of knowledge and skills needed to perform effectively. This situation generates some degree of nervousness and anxiety and will contribute to learning difficulties if the supervisor makes no attempt to minimize this legitimate anxiety. Research conducted by Gomersall and Myers indicates that during the initial time on a new job, employees experience a high degree of anxiety that is disruptive to their ability to learn.[1] Gomersall and Myers found not only that the first few days on a new job are anxious and disturbing, but also that initiation practices by other employees are the primary cause of the anxiety. In addition, they found that new employees are reluctant to discuss problems with supervisors, and, finally, that turnover by newly hired employees is most often caused by anxiety.

Bienvenu indicates that new employees "feel that they are going through a trial period and their status is in jeopardy; therefore, they will refrain from giving any indication which may appear to them to be a threat to their job security."[2] As a result, they will be reluctant to ask questions, and they may also respond as though they understand something when in fact they are uncertain or unclear. This creates a problem later when the supervisor or trainer feels that new employees are either inattentive or slow learners because they are unable to recall information or to perform a task already explained. Instead, the cause of the learning problem may be the training environment if a person was not assured that it was all right to ask questions and to cover material more than once or twice to acquire the necessary expertise.

Negative and Positive Feelings. Feelings of anxiety are too often joined by other negative feelings during an employee's first weeks on a new job. When thinking about early job experiences, most people recall with greater clarity the negative aspects of those situations. While there are certainly positive feelings that individuals may recall about their initial experiences on a new job, negative feelings tend to dominate. These negative feelings include anger, stupidity, fear, hostility, hopelessness, resentment, disorientation, self-consciousness, boredom, and insecurity. Obviously, these feelings are not ones from which a new employee can build self-confidence or self-esteem about the job or cultivate a positive outlook about the work environment. These negative feelings also get in the way of learning, because the new employee will be distracted by emotion and not be able to listen or comprehend well.

Feelings essential to the learning environment include curiosity, optimism, enthusiasm, pride, and a sense of challenge. The challenge to super-

1. Earl R. Gomersall and M. Scott Myers, "Breakthrough in On-the-Job Training," *Harvard Business Review* 44 (July–Aug. 1966):64.

2. Bernard J. Bienvenu, *New Priorities in Training: A Guide for Industry* (New York: American Management Assn., 1969), p.37.

visors is to establish an environment in which positive, not negative, feelings will be generated. It is through these positive feelings that employees are likely to develop a sense of commitment to their work, a strong sense of their own value to the library, and a willingness and ability to adapt to change. Therefore, supervisors and trainers should observe the work environment to see whether the new employee is being welcomed to the department by other staff and receiving assistance and general support, or whether "initiation" practices exist by the old staff for the new. If the new employee doesn't "survive" the initial orientation and training and thus resigns, then it will create more work for everyone. The recruitment process must begin again, training must be repeated, and other staff have to carry the additional workload until the position is filled and the person trained. Overall, the morale of the department suffers in this type of environment.

Of course, not all unhappy or disgruntled employees resign. Many continue their employment while displaying poor performance over the years because of a low commitment to the work and to the library. Too often, new employees are lost as productive members of the library staff, but they may remain on the payroll until their retirement. For new employees or employees transferred to a new position, supervisors can take a number of steps to build a positive training experience. They can assure that a comfortable working environment exists, that meaningful working relationships among staff are encouraged, that mechanisms for communication within the unit and the library are explained, that expectations regarding performance during and after training are clarified, and that expectations for behavior other than task-related ones are explained and discussed. Training should also be fitted to the individual as much as possible. The supervisor should review the person's application, information obtained from the job interview, and references in order to weigh the abilities and attitudes that the person will bring to the new job.

One final observation about the new employee training situation that should be addressed here has to do with the new employee who has held the same or a similar position in another organization. Too often in this situation, most especially with professionals, the supervisor assumes that these individuals do not need training, that they are experienced, and that they will pick up everything on their own. These assumptions are erroneous, because while experience is valued (indeed it probably was a strong factor in hiring a person), any new staff member needs support and direction in learning about a new environment. So when planning training for the new employee, one should not restrict attention to only the person who has minimal work experience. Clearly, the training program should be adjusted for more experienced persons so that they are not bored by unnecessary review or inhibited from assuming full responsibilities as soon as possible. When hiring an experienced person, the supervisor should conduct a review with the new employee on the first day of employment to discuss the person's background and strengths with regard to knowledge, skills, and abilities. This review with the new employee will signal that the supervisor sees previous experience as valuable and worthwhile but at the same time is not making assumptions about the depth or extent of experience.

With any new employee, the supervisor has a unique opportunity to establish the foundation for a productive working relationship by recognizing the importance of the training experience to the individual.

Performance Improvement

Every supervisor will occasionally face the need for retraining staff when performance problems develop. A performance problem is represented by a discrepancy or gap between the supervisor's expectations for performance (quality, quantity, or the behavior expressed when carrying out tasks or duties) and the employee's performance. The supervisor will be concerned with "closing the gap" between established performance expectations or standards and the individual's performance. There may be a number of reasons why experienced staff will require training:

> They prefer the "old" way of doing something and simply revert,
> They may be getting bored and are not as attentive,
> They may make minimal use of certain knowledge or a set of skills, and so they simply forget.

As there are a number of factors that may contribute to poor performance, the first step for the supervisor is not to rush into retraining the staff member but to analyze the performance problem to determine its exact nature, its scope, whether it is serious enough to warrant correction, and the appropriate mechanism for correcting or minimizing it. Supervisors also should refrain from attributing a motive to the employee. Too often, a supervisor may jump to conclusions about the "why" of poor performance before even determining the extent of the problem. It is not unusual to hear a supervisor say that "George has a bad attitude," or that "Samantha is lazy," or blame numerous other attributes for performance problems. If a supervisor moves from identifying a problem to ascribing motivation to the employee, barriers are erected that will prevent the supervisor from seeing the problem clearly or from being committed to work with the employee to correct the situation. After all, if a supervisor thinks that Samantha is lazy, then he or she will see

Samantha as hopeless and not be inclined to "waste" time on her. The supervisor has now potentially created an even bigger problem than may have existed with Samantha's performance; Samantha has been sent a signal that the supervisor has given up on her. The employee may not even know why, but she will probably fulfill the supervisor's opinion at this point and not make an effort to correct the performance problem. Supervisors should seek a way to break this type of cycle that reinforces negative feelings about the work environment. They should develop an analytical approach in order to assess performance problems and to identify potential solutions. At the same time, there needs to be an honest commitment to wanting to see the person improve his or her performance. Too often, supervisors describe problem situations as the "problem employee," which polarizes a situation very quickly. The employee who realizes that he or she is viewed as a problem employee is going to be discouraged, angry, and defensive. These negative feelings will not help the supervisor in seeking improvement. On the other hand, if the supervisor approaches the employee by focusing on the situation created by poor or inadequate performance, the employee will be more likely to respond in a positive way to suggestions and assistance from the supervisor to improve performance.

The following outline adapted from Mager suggests an analytical process that supervisors can use in assessing performance problems in order to determine their scope, seriousness, and cause.[3]

1. Describe the specifics of the problem. How do you know that there is a problem? Is the information reliable?
2. Is correcting the problem worth the time and energy? What would happen if the problem were ignored?
3. Does the employee know that his or her performance is unsatisfactory? Have performance responsibilities and standards been communicated clearly? Has the fact of unsatisfactory performance been discussed?
4. Are there obstacles preventing the employee from performing satisfactorily? Consider obstacles such as interruptions, lack of necessary equipment or materials, lack of cooperation from other staff, and lack of knowledge or skill.
5. Has the employee performed the duties or tasks in a satisfactory manner previously? Is the employee capable of performing work if he or she wants to do so?
6. Are the rewards and punishments for performance clear so that the employee is not rewarded for poor performance?

3. Robert F. Mager and Peter Pipe, *Analyzing Performance Problems, or "You Really Oughta Wanna"* (Belmont, Calif.: Fearon, 1970).

7. Are there personal problems that exist that are interfering with the person's ability to perform?
8. Are the expectations for performance reasonable?

Depending on the answers to these questions, the supervisor will recognize a number of actions, ranging from training to disciplinary action, that need to be taken in order to address performance problems.

If training is the logical response to the performance gap, then there are some specific considerations for retraining staff. One of the first issues that the supervisor should consider is how to provide retraining for the employee in a positive and supportive manner. How does the supervisor prevent the person from feeling embarrassed or humiliated in front of co-workers because of the retraining? Also, what reasonable expectations and standards should be set to measure successful completion of the training? Will continued employment depend on successful retraining? These issues should be discussed with the appropriate trainers prior to laying out a training plan for the employee, and there should be agreement that the intent is to assist and help the person. It will be important to convey to the employee that the supervisor believes that he or she has the capability to perform the work, and that training is a legitimate way to provide further assistance in order to obtain the desired performance level.

Retraining a staff member who has exhibited performance problems can be difficult, and the supervisor and trainer should recognize all of the pitfalls before they start training, in order to avoid them whenever possible. Indeed, if supervisors acknowledge that retraining will occur from time to time—that it is part of normal operations—then their reaction to the person who needs to be retrained will be more positive and supportive.

Operational Problems or Changes

There will be occasions when a supervisor will need to provide training for a number of staff rather than just one individual. This occurs when: (1) problems exist with operations that relate to the performance of many or all of the departmental staff, and (2) changes occur in operational policies, procedures, equipment, or programs. In the first case—operational problems—the process discussed in the previous section for analyzing a performance problem should be used.

Again, the supervisor needs to be careful not to move too quickly from identification of a problem to identification of a solution. This could result in wasted effort and confusion if the real problem is something other than what was initially identified or if a solution is inadequate for the scope of the problem. When operational problems appear to involve more than one individual in a department, then more information should be obtained in order to interpret accurately the extent or scope of the problem situation.

The problem may be fairly straightforward, such as when all of the night staff at the circulation desk are not following closing procedures. Since the problem involves a matter of procedure, no doubt written guidelines issued to all staff would be sufficient to clarify the procedures for them. A more involved situation might be one in which some of the staff are having difficulties in understanding how to handle the priority for issuing study carrel keys for half-day usage. In addition, they are encountering problems in dealing effectively with angry or impatient users regarding the study carrel policies. In this case, the supervisor should consider a review of the written policy and procedures to be sure that they are clear, but he or she also should schedule a training session to provide instruction in techniques for working with the public. The intent is to improve the effectiveness of service by considering what weaknesses exist in the information, knowledge, and skills of the staff. The supervisor should approach the training in a non-threatening and non-accusatory manner by indicating that the situation provides an opportunity to improve training while the staff work together to clarify and correct the performance and service problem.

The other situation requiring training for a large number of staff relates to *changes* that occur in various aspects of daily operations. The degree of change in most libraries has accelerated in the past decade, and all signs indicate that this trend will continue. During any one period of time, say six months, change for the individual employee may be minimal (e.g., a change in routine policy or procedure), or it might be a sweeping change (e.g., the implementation of an automated online circulation system). Both situations require attention to the training of staff so that staff are capable of accepting and responding in a positive and skilled manner to the new requirements of their positions and work environments.

An assumption all too frequently made by supervisors when implementing change in a library department is that it is obvious to the staff what needs to be done and that they will be able to learn or to absorb the new requirements without any organized training. This assumption occurs even with supervisors who normally provide a supportive, well-organized training process for new employees. The supervisor mistakenly believes that the current staff do not really need training, just information. In order to be effective in implementing change in the work environment, it will be important to communicate information about the change to staff and to involve those who will be affected by the change as early as possible in discussions—no matter how small or global the change. The more understanding that staff have regarding the reason for the change, the options that have been considered, and the anticipated outcome, the more they will respond in a positive way to this impact on their work life. It is important to involve the staff so that the change is *their* change. People are not as resistant to change *per se* as they are to change that they perceive as forced upon them or over which they have no control or influence.

Supervisors and trainers need to develop an understanding of why staff resistance toward change develops and how they can constructively respond to the resistance. People resist change for a number of reasons, not the least of which is that known routines are comfortable, and new requirements or processes may result in loss of control. Employees feel that in a new environment or under new job requirements, they will have to prove themselves once again and have to demonstrate that they can be successful in their jobs. This environment understandably generates anxiety that is similar to what the new employee feels. Staff may also feel that they will lose something of value if they change. This fear is experienced particularly by staff who have made an investment to a certain way of performing tasks over a long period of time; for them to change is to reject the past. Supervisors have to find a way to express to staff the value of what has been done in the past while establishing a value for the changed situation.

Few staff resist change simply because they want to be difficult. However, they do not necessarily see that they are putting up barriers either. They have probably developed a rationale for their objections to or for their avoidance of the change. In certain environments where the change is very dramatic—introduction of an automated system, redefinition of job assignments among groups of employees, or provision of new services or deletion of old services—staff may feel that their jobs are threatened. Job security is an important issue for any employee. When information is not provided about job reorganization or when major changes are planned for the library or for a department, staff will imagine the worst. Even if jobs will be reduced or eliminated, it is better to inform the staff and to begin planning with the affected individuals for alternative employment. Concern about job security may not be stated by any staff member, but it is often at the root of negative staff response to a changing environment.

In his research on the effects of the introduction of OCLC into academic libraries, Luquire found that the relationship between job security and the evaluation of OCLC by the staff was one of the strongest associations in the study.[4] The more "emphasis placed on job security by the library administration during all phases of the planning, introduction, and arrival of the

---

4. Wilson Luquire, "Attitudes Toward Automation/Innovation in Academic Libraries," *Journal of Academic Librarianship* 8 (Jan. 1983):347.

innovative system,'' the more positive the response of staff. Luquire also found a ''positive relationship between the amount of preparatory technical training and the overall evaluation of OCLC. As the amount of training increased, so did the evaluation [improve].''

Each of the training situations reviewed earlier provides a different dynamic and therefore requires a somewhat different approach by the supervisor and trainer(s). The attention given to the various requirements in the different training situations should pay off with improved results.

Exercise

The supervisor should review each of the three primary situations for which training will be required—new employee, performance problems, and operational problems or changes—and complete the following.

New Employee: What position do you currently have vacant in your department or can anticipate having open in the next few months based on past experience with turnover?

List the factors that you think contribute to a positive training environment in your department.

List any factors that you believe may be negatively influencing the training process in your department.

Performance Improvement: What employee in your department is currently not meeting your performance expectations or standards? Review the questions in the text adapted from Mager's performance analysis to identify possible causes. What steps will you take, and within what time frame, to address this problem?

Operational Problems: Are there any department-wide problems in your department related to staff knowledge, skills, or attitudes, that you would like to see addressed? Use the same steps indicated above to analyze the problem, and then identify the steps that you might take to improve the situation.

Operational Changes: Has there been any change in your department over the past six months for which no training was provided that still may need to be addressed?

Looking ahead for the next six to twelve months, what operational changes can you anticipate for which training will need to be provided? What staff will be affected by these changes? What training will be required in relation to job functions?

3

PLANNING FOR TRAINING

This chapter focuses on specific steps that supervisors should take in planning for effective job training. Training staff is expensive. If training results in desired performance, then the investment of time and energy has been worth it. If training is ineffective, then the dollars associated with training are wasted, and additional funds must be spent to retrain the same employee or to train another employee. Therefore, the supervisor benefits by planning for training rather than haphazardly or casually approaching it. Initial planning for training requires a commitment of time and effort from the supervisor that may not have been devoted to this activity in the past; but once the initial planning has been completed, it will be possible to easily modify and update what already has been developed for the same position when subsequent training is required. In addition, supervisors' skills in planning for training will be strengthened with practice, thus reducing the amount of time demanded for future training efforts.

As supervisors plan training, they will appreciate the difficulty of training well. They will become more aware of the reasons why employees have difficulty understanding certain concepts, techniques, work flow, or procedures. When this perspective is acquired, the supervisor should be able to identify training methods that will assist the employee with the learning process. There are steps in planning that a supervisor can follow to make training a success both for the trainee and for the supervisor.

Job Analysis

The first step in planning for training is to identify the results that are wanted from the job. In assessing the desired results, a supervisor should ask a number of questions, including the following:

> What is it that I want accomplished by the person in this job?
>
> How does the job support the goals of the department?
>
> Does it still meet primary and critical needs?
>
> What is the most effective and efficient way for this work to get done?
>
> What do I want done differently from what has been done in the past in this job?
>
> Am I satisfied with the quality of the work and with the way it was carried out?

In this analysis, the supervisor is asking "What is the product wanted from this job?" Drucker says that to "start with the task rather than the end product may result, . . ., in beautiful engineering of work that should not be done at all."[1] He goes on to say that "one cannot . . . assume that the end product is rational, systematic, consistent. . . . Anyone who starts out with an analysis of the final product, the work itself, will soon find himself asking the question 'Why do we do this and why do we do that?' Usually there is no answer other than, 'We have always done it.'" Certainly this response is heard far too often in libraries, particularly when new staff ask "Why?" The process of work analysis will assist the supervisor in considering what changes should be made in work assignment, work flow, work procedures, or even in specific activities or services. Therefore, an analysis of work is appropriate in several circumstances: prior to filling a position; in addressing a performance problem; or when implementing a change in procedure or service.

Although job training is costly, it is even more so if staff are trained to perform tasks that are no longer valid, that are inefficient, or that unnecessarily duplicate tasks performed by others. While work analysis may not be conducted every time there is a job vacancy, it should be conducted frequently enough so that the supervisor is assured that the available human resources are being used for the most critical needs of the department. It is important to avoid standing on a treadmill repeating what was done yesterday without thought of today or tomorrow. Once

1. Peter S. Drucker, *Management: Tasks, Responsibilities, Practices* (New York: Harper & Row, 1985), p.201.

the supervisor has reviewed the work that needs to be accomplished, then specific analysis of job tasks is the next step.

Analysis of job tasks is necessary to provide the supervisor with specific information about job content and responsibilities. The supervisor needs to identify:

> All job tasks
> Percentage of time to be spent on the individual tasks
> Critical tasks in the job as represented by those for which satisfactory performance *must* be maintained at all times
> Knowledge, skills, and abilities needed to perform each task.

Benedict and Gherman indicate that task analysis identifies both functional and specific job requirements.[2] They define functional job requirements as those "expected of an employee on the first day in the position. They are interpreted as the minimum hiring requirements for the job. Specific skills, knowledge, and abilities enable the employee to perform a specific technology or procedure. Generally, they are acquired through on-the-job experience and training." Job analysis requires that all pieces that make up the total job be considered. Certain tasks or duties may look fairly insignificant to the experienced person but not to the novice who will be trained. The unknown, the unexpected, and the unexplained contribute to the anxiety of the trainee. A task approach to job analysis will give the supervisor job information in manageable units, provide detailed information about job requirements as well as about the tools and resources needed to perform each task, and identify the most complex work within a job. With this level of detailed job information, the supervisor can make changes as desired in the job assignment as well as be better prepared for planning job training. Only a supervisor has the authority to change job assignments or the priorities of job tasks; job analysis therefore should not be delegated to other staff.

Identifying Job Tasks. The supervisor must think about the job and what it entails. If a job description exists, it should be used; if it does not, the review process should generate a current job description. The supervisor will need to ask "What does the person in this job do on a 'normal' day?"; "How will the person spend his or her time?"; and "What are the demands that occur only periodically?" The supervisor, if fairly removed from the job, may need to actually "walk through" some of the job duties in order to get as much detail as possible both on tasks and on

2. F. C. Benedict and P. M. Gherman, "Implementing an Integrated Personnel System," *Journal of Academic Librarianship* 6 (Sept. 1980):211.

requirements. Once the supervisor has developed a complete list of job tasks, it is a good idea to ask other staff who perform the same job to review the task list to suggest modifications.

Identifying Percentage of Time. Once a comprehensive list of job tasks has been compiled, the percentage of time should be estimated for each job task. The estimate of time allocated to job activities is usually built on a work week. This time frame will be sufficient for many jobs, but occasionally a job cycle is such that a number of tasks are performed only on a periodic basis. For instance, supervisors who must prepare monthly or annual reports, conduct performance evaluations, or recruit and train will not perform these tasks on a weekly basis but on a different cycle or as needed. Nonetheless, it is important to make an estimate of the time demands presented by such activities. By estimating percentages of time anticipated to be spent on specific activities, the supervisor is establishing priorities for the employee's time and energy. Determining percentages is important so that the employee knows what is expected; otherwise the person may develop his or her own priorities among job tasks. In many library settings, supervisors may be expected to indicate percentage of time for the purpose of recruitment or classification of positions, but many fail to provide this same information to the employee performing the duties.

Identifying Critical Tasks. The critical tasks are those that have the greatest impact on the department. The critical tasks may not be the ones on which the employee spends the largest percentage of time. Nonetheless, the critical tasks are the ones for which a satisfactory performance must be maintained at all times. These tasks are seen by the supervisor as the ''make or break'' tasks; they are the ones that if performed in the defined manner will ensure continued employment and, conversely, will indicate probable termination if performance is unsatisfactory. For instance, a librarian with responsibility for collection development and management will have a number of duties, such as selection, weeding, and budget management. The supervisor of this librarian indicates the level of performance expected for all duties but also indicates that staying within established budget guidelines is the most critical task. The recognition of critical tasks is important in order to give the employee a clear understanding of performance expectations. The training program is focused on helping the employee meet these performance requirements.

Identifying Knowledge, Skill, and Ability. Next, the supervisor moves to identify the three dimensions that are necessary to perform every task:

Knowledge refers to the information and understanding that an employee needs to carry out specific tasks or activities.

Skill refers to the ability to translate that knowledge into performing tasks or activities.

Ability refers to the attitude, self-confidence, commitment, and motivation that a person brings to the job.

Even though specific knowledge, skill, and ability will be duplicated among the various job tasks, it is important to identify the three for each job task in order that none are overlooked.

As knowledge, skill, and ability are identified, the supervisor must also decide of these what the employee should already possess on the first day of employment and what will be provided in training. In some cases, such a clean division may not be possible, and the supervisor, while desiring certain knowledge or skills on the first day of employment, should not assume that all people will indeed have these skills or have them at the level of expertise desired. In any case, it is important to determine whether the employee indeed does have the expected knowledge, skill, and ability.

The following example illustrates a job analysis for two library positions—a clerical position in technical services, and a librarian position in reference.

Example

Library Assistant—Cataloging

General Description:

1. Conducts pre-catalog searching in OCLC for all incoming books in English and Western European languages, and prepares books for either full or brief record cataloging functions per established guidelines.

2. Assists in the maintenance of the Name Authority File, including typing and filing of cards.

3. Provides Subject Authority support, including pulling and correcting cards from the public and subject catalogs. Types cross-reference sheets. Updates LC Classification schedules.

Task: Pre-Catalog Searching

Knowledge	Skill	Ability
English, German, French	Translate bibliographic entries	Work with multiple languages and materials effectively

Knowledge	Skill	Ability
OCLC	Use all required OCLC functions using established guidelines for productivity and error rate	Comfortable with computer system

(and so forth)

Librarian—Reference Department

General Description:

1. Provide service at the reference desk—typically 12 to 15 hours per week—giving direct assistance to library users in identifying materials and services of the library and in use of the same. Specifically provide instruction in the use of bibliographic tools.

2. Process interlibrary loan requests received from faculty and graduate students by verifying the bibliographic information before it is forwarded to the ILL staff for processing.

3. Conduct database searches for faculty and graduate students following established guidelines.

Task: Reference Desk Service

Knowledge	Skill	Ability
reference collection	interpersonal	patient
general collection	analytical	pleasant
library services and policies	conduct reference interview	friendly
	instruction	assertive
	communication clear/concise	

(and so forth)

By recognizing each of these three components and the relationship among knowledge, skill, and ability, the supervisor will be more likely to identify the appropriate content, focus, approach, and sequence for training. While the process, to this point, will provide a wealth of information on which to build an effective training plan, there is still more to be done to increase the likelihood of successful training.

Exercise

1. Identify a position that is currently vacant or that you anticipate will become vacant in the next six months or so.

2. Analyze the work that is performed in this position, asking questions such as: what is it that I want accomplished by this job; how does the job support the goals of the department, and does it meet critical needs; what is the most effective and efficient way for this work to get done; what do I want done differently from what has been done in the past; am I satisfied with the quality of the work or the way it is carried out?

Write down responses to these questions, and determine what changes you will want to make in the position as a result of this analysis.

3. Now, identify all of the tasks associated with the job, the percentage of time spent on each individual task, what the critical tasks are for the job, and the knowledge, skill and ability needed to perform each task.

It helps to organize the material in the following way:

Task   Knowledge   Skill   Ability

4. Identify those competencies that you expect the person to already possess—the ones that will not be included in job training.

Performance Standards

Though performance standards are not unknown in libraries, they tend to have been developed most often for those positions for which requirements can be measured quantitatively by amount produced and error rate. This focus has meant that most performance standards have been used for general clerical positions or for technical services positions.

Even though a quantifiable measurement is not possible for many library jobs, supervisors still have expectations about the quality of performance. These expectations should be made clear to the staff. If the supervisor does not define performance expectations, then the employee will be unable to strive for what the supervisor wants. Indeed, if a vacuum exists, the employee will establish his or her own standards. Research conducted in the 1930s by Roethlisberger and Dick, referred to as the Hawthorne studies, demonstrated that employees performing the same or similar tasks will always set unofficial guidelines for productivity for the group.[3] Furthermore, they will try to keep everyone in line so that no one drops below or exceeds the group norm for performance. Therefore, if a supervisor fails to define performance expectations, the employees will have free rein to establish, individually or collectively, acceptable performance levels.

Although the supervisor is responsible for establishing performance standards or expectations, staff who actually perform the job tasks should be asked to provide their view of quality and, when appropriate, quantity. A mutual development of performance expectations and objectives is particularly important with professional staff. Even though the staff viewpoint is important, the supervisor has the final responsibility to set the standards. The supervisor should not appear to be relinquishing an expectation if staff will continue to be evaluated against it. "Hidden" expectations or standards should be avoided.

Focusing on Results. In establishing performance standards, the supervisor should focus on the *results* that are wanted from the job. The expected results should be based on the performance of fully trained and knowledgeable staff. To develop performance expectations based on results, the supervisor must ask a number of questions:

> What will the employee be able to do as a result of training?
> How will the employee demonstrate successful achievement? How do I know when performance is unacceptable?

When considering the working environment, the supervisor should ask questions such as the following:

> What are the limitations in the work setting that may affect performance?
> Are there difficult people to work with?
> Will the employee be expected to work independently or within very specific guidelines?

Each supervisor will have other questions to explore as a means of clarifying performance standards and expectations. Some supervisors will undoubtedly respond that the jobs they supervise cannot be measured or evaluated. Although there are library jobs for which writing performance expectations will be difficult, it is possible to do. If the written standards do not result in a measurable statement in every case, at least the supervi-

---

3. F. J. Roethlisberger and W. J. Dick, *Management and the Worker* (Cambridge, Mass.: Harvard University Pr., 1939).

sor will have moved closer to clarifying what is expected in job performance. In discussing the development of performance objectives, Mager states that "intangibles are often intangible only because we have been too lazy to think about what it is we want students to be able to do."[4]

The jobs for which it is most difficult to write specific measurements for performance are those that involve what Drucker terms "knowledge work."[5] This type of work requires mental effort, and the results are typically not readily apparent. For instance, a bibliographer selects materials in a subject area for which he or she has an expertise. How would a supervisor measure the selection process, since it all occurs in the bibliographer's head? In addition, the supervisor may not even have the subject or language expertise to judge the final selections. In these cases, a general statement of performance expectations or objectives should be developed so that the staff member understands what attributes are expected to signal a satisfactory performance. For selection, this might involve a description of several activities, such as responding to faculty requests for materials, keeping abreast of new courses being offered, being aware of and using current selection sources, and managing funds. Drucker indicates the importance of having performance objectives and explains that these should be "clear, unambiguous, measurable results; a deadline; and a specific assignment of accountability."[6] He also interjects, however, that "objectives that become a straitjacket do harm. Objectives are always based on expectations. And expectations are, at best, informed guesses. . . . Objectives are not fate; they are direction."

Whether one uses the term "goals," "objectives," "expectations," or "standards" is not critical; what is important is that employees understand clearly the performance results desired by the supervisor.

Mager indicates that a meaningful objective is one that "succeeds in communicating your intent . . . ."[7] He goes on to say that there are "many slippery words that are open to a wide range of interpretation . . . if you use *only* such broad terms (or 'fuzzies') when trying to communicate a specific instructional intent, you leave yourself open to misinterpretation." Mager then provides the following list of words to contrast the "slippery" words with those less likely to lead to confusion.

4. Robert F. Mager, *Preparing Instructional Objectives*, 2nd ed. (Belmont, Calif.: Pitman Learning, 1975), p.73.

5. Drucker, *Management: Tasks, Responsibilities*, p.176.

6. Ibid., p.101.

7. Mager, *Preparing Instructional Objectives*, p.20.

Words Open to *Many Interpretations*	*Words Open to* *Fewer Interpretations*
to know	to write
to understand	to present
to appreciate	to identify
to grasp	to sort
to believe	to solve
to accept	to construct
to handle	to compare

The following example provides several illustrations of performance expectations, standards, or objectives for library job tasks.

*Example*_____

Library Assistant—Circulation Desk

Task: Assist Users at the Circulation Desk

1. Be on duty as scheduled.
2. Demonstrate knowledge of circulation policies and procedures by providing correct information.
3. Demonstrate familiarity with library services and locations by referring users.
4. Exhibit good communication in clarity of response and pleasant manner toward users.
5. No complaints are received from users about the way they have been served.

Reference Librarian—Reference Desk

Task: Assist Users at the Reference Desk

1. Avoidance of behavior that will create a defensive attitude on the part of the client, such as the use of jargon, arrogance, etc.
2. Non-judgmental manner in responding to all questions.
3. Ability to identify the real questions, and use of probing or follow-up questions as appropriate.
4. Good listening skills, and non-verbal behavior that is positive and not distracting.
5. Ability to answer questions accurately and efficiently based on sound knowledge of the reference collection.
6. Ability to provide information or direction regarding the library's collections, holdings, and locations of materials or services.

7. Ability to provide instruction in the use of sources at the level appropriate for the knowledge or skill of the patron.

Once the supervisor has established performance expectations or standards for the job, it is then necessary to determine what is reasonable to expect during the training process as learning progresses and as the trainee develops confidence.

Exercise

1. Referring to the material covered in this chapter, review task assignments and develop performance standards or expectations for the job for which you are planning training.
2. Now review the job and determine if there exist other performance standards or expectations that do not relate to a specific task but instead relate to the position as a whole. Are there general expectations in terms of how the person will carry out the work? Describe these expectations as well.

While performance standards are supposed to be measurable, it is better to make an attempt to get something down in writing even if initially you are unsure about how you will measure success.

Training Objectives

Training objectives provide the trainee with a specific understanding about what should result from the training process. When developing training objectives—as with defining performance expectations—the focus is on results, and these results should be measurable. Warren states that behavior on the part of the trainee must first "be observable; that is, the potential trainee must do or say something. Second, these observable behaviors must be measurable; we must know when the trainee is acting or communicating correctly and be able to compare his or her performance to that of others or to a standard."[8]

8. Malcolm W. Warren, *Training for Results: A Systems Approach to the Development of Human Resources in Industry* (Reading, Mass.: Addison-Wesley, 1969), p.69.

Mager describes three reasons for developing training objectives: ''First when clearly defined objectives are lacking, there is no sound basis for the selection or design of instructional materials, content, or methods. If you don't know where you're going, it is difficult to select a suitable means for getting there. . . . A second important reason . . . has to do with finding out whether the objective has, in fact, been accomplished. . . . A third advantage of clearly defined objectives is that they provide students with the means to organize their own efforts toward accomplishment of these objectives.''[9] According to Mager, training objectives also cause one to think seriously about what is worth training for, what is worth spending time and effort to accomplish, and, finally, what the basis is for improving the training effort.

Because performance expectations or standards are developed on the basis of fully trained staff, the trainee needs to understand what will be expected both during and at the conclusion of the training effort. For instance, the performance standard for shelving is written for trained shelvers. The trainee needs to know how long he or she will have before having to meet that standard. Another example is the experienced cataloger, who is expected to catalog 100 books a month, while the librarian being trained in cataloging may not be expected to meet that standard for a year. Training objectives also formalize the commitment supervisors make to employees to help them reach the stated objectives.

A training plan should include two types of objectives: a general statement about performance expected at the conclusion of the training period; and training objectives for each segment of the training process. Examples of both of these types of training objectives follow.

Example

General Objective. Cataloger (inexperienced). At the conclusion of the first year as a cataloger, the person will have completed all components of the formal training program. At that time, the person will be able to meet all stated performance standards for original cataloging (including OCLC requirements) for the humanities collection. The person will have a sound grasp of AACR2 and local standards and be able to use the appropriate standards as defined in departmental guidelines. By the end of the first year, the cataloger will be expected to establish and maintain a production rate of ''X'' books cataloged each month.

---

9. Mager, *Preparing Instructional Objectives*, p.6.

A training objective for an experienced cataloger would be somewhat different. In particular, the time line might vary, as well as the expectation of knowledge and skill.

Example

General Objective. At the conclusion of the formal six-month training program, the cataloger should be thoroughly familiar with local modifications to national cataloging practices and be able to apply these within established guidelines as described in the departmental manual. The cataloger should meet the monthly quota of "XY" at the conclusion of this period.

The second type of objective within a training plan focuses on a very specific segment of the training. Such an objective would be written to reflect what is expected at the conclusion of specific training activities so that the trainee knows what is expected as he or she moves through the training process.

Example

Specific Objective. At the conclusion of the bibliographic searching training, the trainee will be expected to conduct pre-order searching on routine English-language materials with no more than three searches returned with errors within a week. At that time, the trainee will continue to conduct, under direct supervision, pre-order searching on French materials and on more difficult English-language materials requiring an increased facility with bibliographic tools. It is expected that the latter will be performed independently within another two months.

By defining the objectives for the training process, the supervisor, trainer, and trainee will all share a common goal and all have a common mechanism for evaluating whether the desired result has been achieved.

Exercise

1. Identify training objectives that you have for specific areas or segments of the job that you have analyzed. What is it you want to accomplish; what results do you expect in performance? Write out these objectives.

2. Consider desired performance over a longer period of time (six months, a year, two years), and identify what you expect to be accomplished at the end of the formal training period and at the end of this longer period of learning. Write out these objectives.

Sequence for Training

At this point, the supervisor should have identified the content of the training based on the job analysis and on having determined what skills and knowledge the person should already possess. Now it is necessary to fashion a whole from these parts so that a natural and logical order exists for presenting the considerable information needed by the trainee. Developing a training plan may seem somewhat overwhelming by this time given all of the information that has been identified; indeed, it might appear as though the trainee will have to learn everything at once. Since such wholesale learning is not possible, the supervisor must establish an order for the training so that the trainee is not confused and is able to proceed through training using knowledge and skills learned at each stage.

To develop this plan, the supervisor will need to go back to the list of tasks to be performed and the chart of the knowledge, skills, and abilities required; he or she then will identify what must be learned first, second, and so forth. The training process should represent a building block concept so that the trainee is always building on what has already been learned. This approach will make it less likely that instruction will be presented before background information has been covered. Thus, confusion will be minimized. For example, an office employee might be expected to answer incoming phone calls, refer the calls both within the office and to other departments, take messages, and provide information. What does the person have to know before anything else is covered? First, the person should understand the phone instrument—how to use hold buttons, how to transfer calls, and the like. Next the trainee will need to know the correct way to answer the phone, information to be gathered when taking messages, and so forth. If the training information is not laid out in a logical sequence, it is possible that an explanation of phone operation might be overlooked. The employee will likely face a problem when trying to transfer a call or put a caller on "hold." This confusion results in frustration for everyone involved. So training for the

3

Discuss how to answer the
phone, take messages, and
respond to inquiries.
Discuss phone manner or
style.

2

Review the phone list with names or
departments.
Identify "important" callers.
Go over the message form.

1

Review the phone instrument and procedures for transferring
calls.

Fig. 1. Task: Answering the Phone

task of answering the phone should be developed conceptually as a stair-
case or set of building blocks (fig. 1).

As the supervisor reviews job tasks and the knowledge, skills, and abilities required, it will be important to identify what activities the trainee
will be asked to perform first. What tasks occur only periodically and
could be covered later in the training process? The foundation of knowledge and skills needed to perform a task must be recognized so that training responds to these needs. For instance, if a reference librarian is expected to perform reference desk service immediately, then training in
this function will be a priority. The tasks related to reference desk service
as well as the knowledge, skills, and abilities needed for the activity are
then identified for training. The training might include a review of departmental guidelines for reference service; discussion with the department head about the library's philosophy of reference service; instruction
in the content and location of the reference collection; instruction in library services and locations; and explanation of the typical reference
needs of patrons.

In addition to determining the sequence for presenting training on
specific tasks, it is necessary to decide when to present information about
the organization; general background about the department, including
its goals and objectives; introductions to staff and to the library facilities,

such as the staff lounge; and department or library procedures for numerous activities ranging from obtaining supplies to requesting vacation time. In addition, it is necessary to consider when library jargon will be reviewed as well as local library or institution nomenclature.

Although the supervisor may find it difficult to determine the sequence for training, it is far more confusing for the employee to make sense out of training or out of the job if there is little or no order.

When developing a sequence for the training process, the supervisor does not yet need to map out a specific schedule with dates and times. Instead, what is needed at this juncture in planning is to define what should occur first in learning so that the trainee will have the necessary background to understand what is being presented at each stage of training.

Exercise

Using the information gathered from the job analysis, it is now necessary to consider the sequence for the job training:

> What skills or knowledge do you expect people to have on their first day on the job? Which do you expect to train them for?
>
> What is the most urgent knowledge or skill(s) that the person must have to function immediately?
>
> What tasks or activities can be learned independently of something else? What tasks or activities are not as urgent to learn in relation to job tasks that need to be performed?

Selecting and Training Trainers

The choice of who will do the training is vital if the process is to be successful, as trainers play a critical role in successful learning. Indeed, an excellent trainer can do much to overcome a poorly organized training program, but a poor trainer cannot create success even from a well-organized training plan. Any staff member who plays a significant role in instructing another employee should be viewed as a trainer, whose skills and ability in this activity should be assessed. Davies states that "far too many [trainers] see themselves as 'knowledge banks,' paid for what they know rather than for what they achieve. Yet in every sense of the term, learning involves *change*, so that the role of an educator and trainer is essentially that of an agent of change."[10] Davies goes on to describe the trainer as being both a "conveyer of new information, and . . . a controller of the social and psychological environment in which . . . learning occurs." In the first capacity, the trainer is primarily concerned with the content of the learning task, and in the second capacity, the effective trainer is concerned with the social and psychological processes.

Characteristics needed for trainers to be successful include the following:

1. Ability to teach knowledge and skill to another person
2. Enjoyment of interacting and sharing knowledge with others
3. Openness to new ideas and suggestions
4. Ability to assess performance
5. Possession of a positive and constructive attitude toward the work, the department, the library, the supervisor, and the co-workers.

Therefore, the most knowledgeable employee in the department may not be the most capable trainer if the other abilities are not present, and not everyone will be an effective trainer. An employee with a poor attitude toward the library is *not* a desirable trainer, regardless of the degree of knowledge or skill possessed. In this situation, the supervisor could have at the end of the training process a well-trained, skilled employee with a bad attitude.

Supervisors should evaluate staff who have training responsibilities and identify improvements that are needed in their training skills. The need to train the trainers should be seen as an opportunity to improve training. The supervisor should describe to trainers his or her expectations for this activity and work actively with trainers to improve both the content and the process of training.

Guidelines for trainers should be developed to clarify expectations and as a means by which to measure successful trainer performance. These guidelines should focus on the trainer's ability to:

Take an interest in the trainee.
Create enthusiasm.
Keep morale high.
Communicate clearly.
Listen.
Provide feedback to the trainee in a timely and supportive manner (praise in public, correct in private).

10. Ivor K. Davies, "Style and Effectiveness in Education and Training: A Model for Organizing Teaching and Learning," *Instructional Science* 1 (March 1972):54.

Recognize the importance of self-confidence and self-esteem in the learning process.

Understand learning principles.

Recognize the value of learning from mistakes.

Staff other than the supervisor can play a valuable role in providing training. The benefits to using staff include adding a breadth of knowledge and experience to the training process, sharing the time requirements for training, providing peers for the trainee to interact with, strengthening working relationships within the department, and encouraging a commitment among co-workers to the success of the trainee. Developing staff as trainers is a valuable way to provide them with additional skills. It is also a mechanism for improving the results of job training.

Exercise

1. What expectations do you have for trainers in your department? Write these down so that you can share them with the trainers.

2. Identify potential trainers in your department as well as those who already are trainers—officially or unofficially.

3. Evaluate each of the individuals as a trainer using the expectations that you have and the information provided in this chapter. Focus particularly on the following traits: communication skills, demonstrated interest in trainees, ability to create enthusiasm and maintain morale, positive attitude toward all aspects of the work and the library, effectiveness at analyzing performance, and ability to plan training.

4. What steps can you take to improve the performance of trainers in your department?

Training Methods

On-the-job training is typically approached in a singular manner consisting of one-on-one instruction with the trainee. While this is effective in certain situations, there are other options available for successful job training. Methods are reviewed in this section to provide supervisors and trainers with alternatives to consider in developing an approach to each training situation.

Demonstration. The method that is most often used in library job training is demonstration. It involves a trainer explaining specific procedures, equipment, and routines to the trainee by demonstrating how a task is carried out, where to locate materials, how to respond in a specific situation, and so forth. Demonstration is a valid training method and is most effective when it is used first by the trainer to show how something is done and then by the trainee to show that he or she has understood and mastered the technique. Demonstration is most effective when it is used in the job setting where the activities and environment represent the exact setting in which the person will actually perform. Demonstration in the work area also allows the trainer to have at hand all of the appropriate equipment, materials, and other resources necessary for training. Because a trainer is available during the training process to make immediate evaluation of performance, this method for training provides an excellent way for observing, correcting, and supporting the trainee as he or she learns. The demonstration method for training also is valuable because it is easy to adapt to the trainee's own abilities and pace. The training process can be easily modified to move more quickly for the experienced or fast learner, and to slow down for someone who is having difficulty with the process.

Demonstration one-on-one training, however, does require a high degree of instructor skill. As Warren points out, "undesired behaviors or unrelated behaviors may be reinforced by an inexperienced instructor or one with more pressing duties."[11] While the method is more personalized and thus suggests that the trainee will get considerable support and assistance, there are two distinct drawbacks. First, it assumes that training is always best presented in the sequence in which a task is performed. This approach may not be effective if background information or a related skill is needed in order to perform a task or tasks. In this case, the sequence of training would not be effective for learning. Second, when all training occurs within the job setting, it may be disruptive to others, since the trainee is learning and thus will be responding more slowly to performing certain routines. In this environment, the trainee is likely to feel pressured and anxious about how he or she is being perceived by co-workers and by the trainer.

Because of the advantages of this training method and the fact that library training is provided most often to individuals rather than to groups, this method will continue to be heavily used. It does require careful planning and identification of skilled trainers or the provision of training for the trainers.

11. Warren, *Training for Results*, p.89.

Lecture. There are many situations in library training when a lecture method might be used either to present a great deal of background information or technical knowledge, or possibly to train a group of people in certain procedures. For instance, if the supervisor of a shelving unit in a college library hires ten or so new students every September for the school year, then a group lecture on reading call numbers for shelving, following procedures for organizing books, and so forth would be an effective way to deliver this information. The advantage of the lecture is to provide a number of people with information in one group. The primary disadvantage is that trainees are passive in this process. They listen, take notes, and possibly ask questions at the end of the presentation. The skills required by the instructor or trainer are not as highly developed as in the individualized setting either. Also, the lecture method is not very adaptable to the various levels of knowledge or learning found among the trainees.

Supervisors can make good use of a lecture approach but should always supplement it with some other training to be sure that the desired behavior to be exhibited in performance has actually been learned. Using the earlier example of the supervisor of the shelving operation, the use of a lecture session to instruct new shelvers in reading call numbers could be followed by a test to determine their level of comprehension. The trainer could have the trainees each organize a group of books in correct order, or index cards with call numbers could be used instead. In this manner the trainer could identify those who will need follow-up assistance in grasping call numbers. In addition, when training staff for a number of tasks, the lecture approach should be used only sparingly because it becomes tedious for the trainee and diminishes learning when trainees are not actively involved.

Discussion. To provide certain background information and ideas to trainees, a discussion method is the most valuable. This is particularly true when the supervisor wishes to discuss with trainees organizational information, such as library and department objectives and priorities, and communication or performance expectations. There are two different types of discussion that might be used: structured and unstructured. In a structured discussion, the trainer outlines the content and determines the issues to be covered. Although the trainee participates in the discussion, it is the trainer who determines the focus and course of the discussion. An example of a structured discussion would be training a new supervisor to handle recruitment activities. The department head has very specific objectives, such as informing the new supervisor of specific policies and procedures, emphasizing the importance of the recruitment process in maintaining good relations with the community, establishing the priority of selecting staff who are well-suited to the job and to the library, and describing the expectations regarding affirmative action. In this setting, the discussion is structured by the department head (or the head of personnel) and is intended to answer questions, review policies, and provide procedural information. The trainee should understand in advance what the content and focus will be in the discussion and what is expected to result from the session. This approach is used a great deal in libraries without being recognized as part of training. It should be acknowledged as a training method so that the training objectives can be identified. A structured discussion is very useful if the desired learning of the trainee can be evaluated based on verbal responses. The structured discussion relies on a trainer who is skilled in managing the personal interaction between the trainer and the trainee(s). Not every trainer can handle this situation effectively.

The second type of discussion is the unstructured, and, as its name implies, it is a method that is primarily directed by the trainees. This method uses more of a conference approach, whereby the trainees identify the topics or issues, and the trainer serves to facilitate the discussion or to provide clarification if necessary. This type of training is most appropriate when judgment will have to be regularly exercised in performance; for instance, job activities that rely on the interpretation of policies or procedures or on the interpersonal style of the staff member benefit from this method. In these situations, the trainer may want the trainee to explore alternatives for responding to situations rather than follow a specific guideline. An unstructured discussion might be used in training reference librarians on selecting certain sources in response to a particular reference question. The discussion would focus on having the trainee explain how he or she might respond to the question and then explain his or her rationale for the response. The same approach could be used to analyze the skills needed in the reference interview or focus specifically on how to behave in response to difficult patron situations. The intent would be to get the trainee to explore and analyze options for performance. This training method has less value for many job training situations, but nonetheless it is worthwhile to consider using the method for certain techniques that must be learned.

Programmed Instruction. Libraries have not made great use of programmed instruction even though there are many job tasks that could be effectively presented in this format. Programmed instruction provides information to trainees in small segments and allows them to check their own progress in learning against ''self-tests'' that are part of the materials. The trainee can review and repeat the materials multiple times until the desired learning or behavior has been achieved. Warren describes programmed instruction as a "system for bringing about behavior change with an extremely high degree of training feedback and response measurement."[12] Programmed instruction can be developed in written format or by using a computer to develop computer assisted instruction.

Programmed instruction can have a high cost associated with the development of the materials and the need to validate these materials prior to use. It does, however, provide independence to the trainee in learning certain types of functions or tasks, which in turn frees the time of the trainer. Supervisors should begin to explore ways in which they can use a programmed instruction approach, whether using paper or machine products, for training in certain functions. For instance, training shelvers in call numbers; or teaching circulation functions, including online systems; or teaching a host of other routine procedures and activities within libraries could be provided with programmed instruction. Programmed instruction is an untapped resource for libraries to increase effectiveness and efficiency in training.

Role Play. Although many library staff have participated in role play situations, it has almost always been when attending a workshop outside of the job environment. Role play, though, can be valuable in job training to prepare staff to respond effectively to a particular type of situation. It would be inadequate simply to describe certain situations (e.g., the threatening patron) and expect that the trainee would then have the anticipated behaviors to respond effectively. Role play allows the trainer to establish a "drama" to depict a real-life situation that the trainee is likely to encounter. In addition, it allows the trainer to establish behavior expectations for responding to specific situations. Role play can have a real value in a number of situations, such as preparing security staff to deal with disruptive patrons; setting performance expectations for circulation or reference staff in responding to unpleasant patron encounters; training reference librarians to conduct a reference interview; or preparing instructional librarians for classroom teaching. Role play is a useful tool not only in formal workshops but also as a training method that every supervisor can use where there is a need to establish and reinforce specific behaviors and for trainees to analyze their own behavior.

The development of role play materials can be costly, although there are sources in the library literature that can be drawn on by supervisors.[13]

12. Ibid.

13. Mildred H. Lowell, *Library Management Cases* (Metuchen, N.J.: Scarecrow Pr., 1975); Mildred H. Lowell, *The Management of Libraries and Information Centers* (Metuchen, N.J.: Scarecrow Pr., 1968); Thomas J. Galvin, *The Case Method in Library Education and In-Service Training* (Metuchen, N.J.: Scarecrow Pr., 1973).

In addition, the trainer will need to be skilled in using the role play approach so that the trainee does not feel embarrassed or awkward. Finally, the trainer must be able to reinforce the appropriate behavior and assist trainees in analyzing their performance in order to see where changes should be made.

Case Study. The case study is often a part of formal workshops developed for managers and supervisors. This method can also provide the supervisor or trainer with a useful opportunity to present the trainee with a complicated situation in advance of its occurring, and then evaluate the trainee's skills and ability to respond correctly. The case study method is built on the use of a well-documented description of a real-life situation. The trainee is expected to take all of the material presented, analyze the information, and present a recommendation for action. This approach allows the trainee to work independently on a problem, to draw on his or her resources, and to practice dealing with complex situations that typify what will be encountered on the job.

This method could be used effectively in preparing a new supervisor in the process of writing a performance evaluation. Other types of situations also exist, particularly for training supervisors, for which the case study could be used effectively. For instance, the handling of a personnel situation, or the writing of a report, or the resolution of a conflict in a committee meeting could all be enhanced by the use of case study materials. This method focuses on the development of analytical and writing skills and therefore is more appropriate for training supervisory and professional staff.

The costs of this method are primarily related to the development of materials, although, as with role play materials, resources are available in the literature.

Selecting a Training Method. Multiple training methods could be considered for library training. Warren outlines the following criteria to consider in selecting a training method:

> Training criteria
> Trainee response and feedback
> Instructor skill level and feedback
> Approximation to the job
> Adaptability to trainee differences
> Cost.[14]

Warren goes on to state that the selection of a training method should consider such questions as "How easily can the instruction be delivered

14. Warren, *Training for Results*, p.82.

in terms of logistical and scheduling problems? How easily can the quality of instruction be maintained using the method? How acceptable is the method to the trainees . . .?"[15]

Selecting training methods requires establishing a balance in the training process. Innovative methods for training should not exceed a department's ability to be successful in using them, nor should traditional approaches be relied on when they clearly do not meet the learning requirements of particular jobs or the needs of trainees.

Exercise

1. Consider the training in your department and identify what training methods are most frequently used. Do you think that the most most frequently used method is effective?

2. In considering the job for which you will want to plan training in the near future, which of the training methods could be effectively used in relation to specific job duties or tasks? Use the following chart to assist you in assessing appropriate training approaches:

Training Approaches	Job Task	Job Task	Job Task	Job Task
Demonstration				
Lecture				
Discussion:				
Structured				
Unstructured				
Programmed				
Instruction				
Role Play				
Case Study				

Writing the Training Plan

At this point, the supervisor has completed all of the background work necessary to develop the written training plan: analysis of the job, establishment of performance standards, identification of content of training and training objectives, determination of sequence of training, identification of trainers, and choice of training methods.

15. Ibid., p.99.

The final step is relatively straightforward, because the supervisor is now going to organize all of the information he or she has accumulated into a training plan that will act as a roadmap or blueprint for the trainer and trainee(s), as well as for the supervisor. All staff involved in the training process should receive a copy of the training plan, including the trainee. In addition, it is recommended that a copy of the training plan be placed in the staff member's personnel file so that there is a record of the training provided.

The training plan should include the training objectives, the content, the sequence, the length of the training process, the names and titles of the trainers, and the location of training if it varies.

Tips on Writing Training Plans. At this point, the supervisor will have a considerable amount of information that must be organized into a single planning document. The following suggestions might be helpful in organizing the material:

> Be specific in describing what will occur in training and the results wanted.
> Provide background information in separate handouts.
> Use action verbs in describing training and desired results.
> Describe activities or training components in positive terms rather than negative ones.
> Consider how to address desired attributes or behaviors that will not be covered formally in training, such as working as part of a team, taking initiative, and working cooperatively with co-workers.

The sample training plans contained in the Appendix should be helpful in understanding formats and approaches.

Limitations of Training Plans. It would be naive to assume that training plans will have no disadvantages at all. Supervisors should be aware of what potential disadvantages exist so that they can guard against them in implementing training plans.

First, a training plan cannot be all-inclusive. The supervisor will have to recognize and alert the trainee to the fact that some aspects of learning about the job or the department will not have been included and that situations or new developments will occur requiring a shift in the plan. It is simply not possible to write down everything about all facets of a job, and this fact should be acknowledged in using a training plan.

Additionally, a training plan can be seen as inflexible by any of the people using it, which can become a liability. The plan should be seen as a guide or a road map, but one that will need to be reviewed, updated, and altered as circumstances dictate. Changes may occur due to activities in the department, such as staff being unavailable due to illness, equipment being out of order, or a new project deadline having been established. Changes in the plan also may be necessary because of the pace of learning of the trainee or because the supervisor overestimated a reasonable pace for learning. If the plan is seen as flexible, then having a plan should not limit or inhibit creativity on the part of a trainer or trainee in accomplishing the learning required. What is important is that everyone see the training plan not as a permanent document that cannot be altered, but as a dynamic one.

A training plan may give a supervisor, trainer, or trainee a false sense of security in the training process because a written document exists. In order to avoid this pitfall, a continuous review process should be established to determine if the existing training plan is reasonable and if it is being followed.

Finally, a trainee may be overwhelmed by a training plan and have reservations about his or her ability to accomplish everything that is described. To avoid this situation, it is important that the supervisor review the training plan initially, explaining the purpose of the plan, the flexibility of the plan, and the points of review. If the trainee understands that there will be support for him or her in moving through the training process and that there is flexibility, he or she will be less likely to feel overwhelmed; indeed, the trainee may be reassured to know that the training has been thought through and planned for.

These potential drawbacks of training plans are not reasons for avoiding an organized approach to training but simply remind us that any approach contains certain limitations.

While the time and energy required to plan for training are considerable, the results that can be achieved are well worth this investment. Through well-planned training, supervisors will not only see an improvement in performance results, but they will also be able to identify a difference in commitment and motivation from employees. Effective training is an investment for the future through staff.

Exercise

1. Write a training plan for the position that you have identified. The plan should contain all of the elements covered in this chapter.

2. Once you have completed the plan, ask several people in the department to review it to see if anything has been overlooked.

3. A week or so before the training is to begin, set a definite schedule for the training, indicating dates and times each day for the various segments to be conducted. Usually, setting a schedule one week at a time is advisable, since many changes can occur in a department to alter a schedule.

4. Distribute a copy of the training plan to everyone who will be directly involved in the training activity. In addition, it is helpful to post the plan somewhere for other staff in the department to see so that they will be aware of when training is being conducted.

4

IMPLEMENTATION OF TRAINING

Once the supervisor has organized the content and sequence of the training, and defined the training objectives, a significant aspect of planning for training has been completed. Implementation of training, however, is the major challenge facing the supervisor and trainer. At this point, the supervisor should focus on the needs of the individuals to be trained. How will trainees be integrated into the department; what skills and abilities will they bring to their work? The supervisor's attention should focus on the process of training and on how, through that process, the trainees will learn responsibility, feel successful, take pride in their work, and develop a sense of commitment toward it. Drucker says that "while managers proclaim that people are their major resource, the traditional approaches to the managing of people do not focus on people as a resource but as problems, procedures, and costs."[1] Supervisors should keep in mind that the training process is a chance to develop a valuable resource, rather than a problem to be faced. At the implementation stage, the needs of the person(s) being trained are the added ingredients that must be considered to assure success.

Motivation

Although concepts or ideas about motivation are familiar to most supervisors, the concepts are seldom considered in the context of staff train-

1. Peter F. Drucker, *Management: Tasks, Responsibilities, Practices* (New York: Harper & Row, 1973), p.308.

ing. Motivation theory, though, is relevant to the training process, since it can provide a clearer understanding of the needs of employees and how these may be addressed during training.

Before World War II, ideas on how to motivate employees focused on two approaches—the "carrot" or the "stick." The carrot approach relied on enticements to urge employees to work faster, with salary being the primary inducement. The stick concept represented punishment or threat, such as termination, poor assignments, undesirable hours, and the like. The carrot and stick approach to motivating people was built on a belief that people basically are lazy and do not want to work, and therefore must be "kicked" or "enticed" forward to produce. Beginning in the late 1940s, research on workers and work environments challenged this concept of people and their attitude toward work. While a great deal has been written about the psychology of workers, including their motivations, achievements, and alienation, there are two primary researchers whose work still provides the foundation of thought and research about motivation. Maslow and Hertzberg developed entirely new concepts regarding the needs of workers. While their approaches to motivation were somewhat different, their conclusions were very similar.

Hierarchy of Needs. Maslow constructed a hierarchy of needs to describe those variables that would motivate employees (fig. 2). His theory is based on two assumptions: first, that needs depend on what a person already has or does not have, and second, that the needs are in a hierarchy of importance. Therefore, within the set of needs that all people have, there is a hierarchy; and as one need is met, another emerges and satisfaction is sought for this new need.[2]

As Maslow suggests, the employee is concerned with basic issues such as pay and health benefits, but once these are minimally met, different needs emerge as represented by the pyramid. Once one set of needs is satisfied, the person naturally begins to focus on other needs. This does not suggest that an employee does not strive to make more money once a salary is secured; indeed, a person may be addressing multiple needs at one time. It does suggest, though, that unless one level is met to a minimal extent, the person is not likely to focus on higher-level needs. Thus, once a desired job with the salary necessary to take care of basic human needs is secured, the person then begins to be concerned with other aspects of employment, such as job security, working relationships, and so forth. An individual is likely to move back and forth on this hierarchy of needs in relation to events occurring in his or her work life.

2. Abraham Maslow, *Motivation and Personality* (New York: Harper & Row, 1954).

SELF-ACTUALIZATION

(becoming what one is capable of becoming)

↑

ESTEEM

(self-esteem, esteem from others)

↑

SOCIAL

(affection, acceptance, friendship, belonging, love)

↑

SAFETY

(security, protection from physical harm)

↑

PHYSIOLOGICAL

(survival, hunger, thirst)

Fig. 2. Maslow's hierarchy of needs. Adapted from Abraham Maslow, *Motivation and Personality* (New York: Harper & Row, 1954).

Satisfiers and Dissatisfiers. Hertzberg developed the motivator-hygiene concept, using Maslow's model of a hierarchy of needs.[3] Hertzberg's model identifies and distinguishes between "satisfiers" and "dissatisfiers" in the work environment (fig. 3). He suggests that six factors contribute to satisfaction and motivation, while other factors are necessary to avoid dissatisfaction among employees.

Hertzberg indicates that certain "critical incidents" occur daily on the job that cause people to feel pleasure or satisfaction with their work. Incidents that contribute to satisfaction are ones through which people feel that they have achieved something worthwhile and ones for which they are recognized and praised.

In developing this concept of motivation, Hertzberg suggests that certain factors will create dissatisfaction or unhappiness for employees when these factors are *absent* from the work environment. However, the existence of these factors at an adequate level will not motivate or satisfy the employee; they will only make the person less dissatisfied. If an employee considers wages or salary to be inadequate, dissatisfaction will result. If

3. Frederick Hertzberg, *Work and the Nature of Man* (New York: World, 1966).

Hygiene Factors	*Motivators*
ENVIRONMENT	JOB ITSELF
Policies and administration	Achievement
Supervision	Recognition for accomplishment
Working conditions	Challenging work
Interpersonal relations	Increased responsibility
Money, status, security	Growth and development
(Dissatisfiers)	(Satisfiers)

Fig. 3. Motivation and hygiene factors. Adapted from Frederick Hertzberg, *Work and the Nature of Man* (New York: World, 1966).

the employee believes the salary to be adequate, then dissatisfaction will no longer exist, but the person will not necessarily be satisfied or motivated.

Hertzberg says that satisfiers and dissatisfiers are not opposites and that what dissatisfies employees will not satisfy them if there is a change in that factor alone. This distinction has important implications for job performance, since it suggests that the factors likely to influence poor performance are different from those affecting acceptable performance. According to Hertzberg, if supervisors want employees to perform at acceptable levels, then they will need to address the "motivator" factors. Motivating factors as defined by Hertzberg correspond to Maslow's need levels of esteem and self-actualization. These are factors that the supervisor can influence beginning with the training process.

Supervisors also need to address issues such as interpersonal relations within the unit and the development of a sense of team work, as well as provide fair and equitable policies, a reward system based on performance results, opportunities for achievement within work, independence in performance, and responsibility, recognition, growth, and development. These many variables are ones that will need to be constantly reviewed and addressed by supervisors and department staff. Supervisors waste energy when they complain about conditions over which they have little or no control, such as salary programs or benefits. Instead, supervisors need to focus on improving the work environment and on developing and rewarding staff. It is in these latter areas that much can be accomplished in relation to staff motivation and morale.

Relevance to the Training Environment. What special relevance does motivation theory have to the training environment, and how will an awareness of such theory assist supervisors and trainers? Primarily, motivation theory provides a context within which supervisors can better understand and even anticipate the needs and behavior of staff during training. During the training process, the supervisor will expect the trainee to be highly motivated—to want to learn, to want to perform. Therefore, a supervisor's recognition of motivation theories is particularly critical at this time. For example, a new employee will be concerned initially with the social needs identified by Maslow: how to fit into the department; how to get along with co-workers and with the supervisor; and what support and assistance will be provided while he or she is learning the job. For instance, if the new person does not meet co-workers immediately and does not understand what other people's responsibilities are or how his or her assignment relates to other people's work and the work flow of the unit, then the person may feel isolated and like an intruder. In such an environment, the trainee is likely to retreat psychologically; he or she will not ask questions and will demonstrate little initiative. This reaction consequently will affect how well an employee learns and performs job responsibilities initially.

In another situation, such as the implementation of an automated circulation system, employees will likely be concerned with ''safety'' needs as represented by job security. Once the new system is installed, will employees still have the same jobs or any jobs at all? Will their pay change? Will they have the appropriate skills to succeed at new tasks? In this situation, the supervisor should recognize that these concerns exist even though they may not be stated openly, and he or she should be sure that they are addressed in a straightforward manner. Schraml points out that the literature reveals that ''some of the major reasons of library and office workers' fear of automation have to do with the threat or reality of job loss, job displacement, reduced opportunities for advancement, and the feeling of human obsolescence.''[4]

Motivation is not something that a supervisor can provide for employees by pushing and pulling them to succeed. Instead, supervisors need to provide an environment in which employees develop a commitment to achieve and pride in their success.

---

4. Mary L. Schraml, ''The Psychological Impact of Automation on Library and Office Workers,'' *Special Libraries* 72 (April 1981):150.

Aspects of Training Requiring Special Attention

Aspects of the training process that require special attention in order to improve training results include communication, training materials, and scheduling of training.

Communication. While effective communication in the work environment is critical at all times, there are specific communication needs that exist during the training process. When effective communication occurs during training, the supervisor will have built a positive foundation for future interactions and interpersonal relations with employees. In considering the many different facets of communication during training, the supervisor needs to recognize that a great deal is being communicated to the trainee both formally and informally. The trainee learns from the instruction provided and also by observing relationships and behavior within the department. Thus, what is communicated during the actual training process (expectations and standards for performance in particular) should be reinforced in practice among all of the employees. There is no point in emphasizing with a new employee that all staff are expected to be on time to work every day if he or she watches other staff regularly come in late without any action being taken. The new employee will accept the norm of the group rather than what he or she has been told. In focusing on specific components of communication during training, the supervisor should not ignore the complex network of communication that proceeds continually in an organizational environment.

There are three dimensions of communication that are particularly important to focus on during training: feedback, training style and methods, and jargon.

Feedback. Communication is an interactive, multi-dimensional act, not a one-way process. So when supervisors are considering the necessary feedback during training they should use the model shown in figure 4. In addition to identifying who will need to be involved in the communication, it is also necessary to recognize that feedback occurs in both formal and informal ways. Feedback on the trainees' progress occurs during the instruction process as the trainer observes responses and performance. In addition, progress should be reviewed in periodic meetings between the supervisor and the trainer, and between the supervisor and the trainee. Periodic review meetings are not often conducted by the supervisor, and yet they are the key to identifying difficulties in training at an early stage and allow the supervisor to provide ongoing support to the trainee. Frequent review meetings allow everyone involved in the training to review

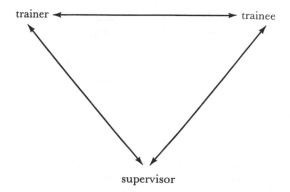

Fig. 4. Communication model for training

progress and any problems. When the training is for a new employee, it is suggested that review meetings be held at least once a week during the first four to six weeks of employment. For other training situations, a similar review process should be established, though the length of time over which it should be conducted will vary depending on the nature of the training. When structuring review meetings, it is suggested that the supervisor meet separately with the trainer and then with the trainee. This procedure will allow both trainer and trainee to speak frankly without being uncomfortable. It should be noted, however, that the trainer should not discuss learning or performance problems with the supervisor that have not been brought to the attention of the trainee. The focus of the review meetings should be to determine if the training is moving at the appropriate pace; if the presentation is clear; and if opportunities for practice, review, and asking questions are being allowed. In addition, the review meeting is a time for the trainee to indicate if sufficient support and encouragement are being provided, and for the supervisor to determine if the trainee's relationship with the trainer is constructive and positive. The supervisor wants to find out how the trainee is feeling about the training, the work, and the department.

Even if the supervisor is the trainer, a review meeting is necessary to provide the opportunity to look at an entire week and to evaluate the trainee's progress. Many frustrations with job training, whether for new employees or for employees learning new routines or operations, could be avoided if supervisors and trainers would periodically review the progress of the trainees, and how the trainers are performing. With new employees, this review sometimes does not occur until several months into their employment or at the end of a probationary period. At that point, it most likely will be too late to correct problems—or at best be very difficult—whereas addressing difficulties early in the training process results more often in positive responses.

In order to achieve constructive and continual feedback, though, more is required than establishing the mechanism for feedback to occur through review meetings. Supervisors and trainers need to recognize what barriers may exist in providing honest and direct feedback to trainees. The difficulties fall into two categories: providing criticism or correction, and providing praise.

What are the reasons why most people find it difficult to provide feedback if it is to correct a problem or indicate dissatisfaction? The reasons tend to relate to concerns about how the trainee will feel about himself or herself and how the trainee will feel about the person providing the correction. Few people feel good if they hurt another person's feelings, nor do they feel good if the person is angry with them. Supervisors need to develop an ability to separate the performance problem from the person; they need to focus the criticism on the desire to see improvement and not cast it in tones that attack the individual. If corrections can be made in this context, the trainee is more likely to accept them in a positive way and not feel defensive or angry. Feedback that may be perceived as negative is also avoided because of a fear that conflict will develop. Unfortunately, conflict is likely to develop if trainees feel they are not provided honest feedback, but the conflict may remain below the surface and as a result not be easy to address. Finally, there is often a concern by supervisors that possibly their criticism is not fair and that their judgment is subjective, and therefore they hesitate to correct a problem or request a change. If supervisors articulate clear performance expectations with trainees, this barrier should be removed or at least reduced.

While providing constructive criticism is difficult to handle effectively, some supervisors also have difficulty in providing praise to staff for good performance. Some of the reasons for this difficulty include the following:

> High expectations exist, and therefore good or excellent performance is not noted.
> Since good performance does not create a problem, it is overlooked.
> Supervisors fear over-praising staff because too much praise will have no value.
> Supervisors want to avoid a perception that there are favorites on the staff.

For these and other reasons, supervisors do not make time to recognize and praise staff for a "job well done." When good performance as well as problems are addressed during training, the trainee will have a good grasp of what is expected. A foundation will then be laid for future discussions of performance, during both formal and informal evaluations.

The consequences of inadequate feedback may be that employee morale drops; the trainee develops negative feelings about himself or herself and the job to fill the vacuum; small problems become crises; staff worry unnecessarily, which interferes with learning; the trainee assumes that he or she is doing well when this is not the case; and opportunities for staff to improve are lost. Constructive and continual feedback should instead contribute to a healthy work environment in which learning and improvement represent a shared value.

Training Style. Trainers have a primary role in and responsibility for effective communication. The ability to share knowledge and information, to listen, to instruct, and to be supportive are all skills that are required by an effective trainer. The trainers' most important communication comes during the actual training sessions when they are explaining, demonstrating, and correcting. There are a number of communication pitfalls that can lead to ineffective results both in learning and in attitude development. Some of these relate to the "false assumptions about training" that were covered in Chapter 1. These false assumptions should be reviewed by every trainer before beginning training.

Trainers often unwittingly say or do things that are damaging to the training process or to the trainee. Such words or actions may not cause an immediate negative reaction but may contribute to a continuing poor relationship between the trainee and the work setting. Several examples of situations trainers should try to avoid follow.

1. *Rushing ahead.* The trainer makes assumptions about what trainees already know or have understood, and moves quickly from the explanation of one task or activity to another. Trainees are not likely to alert the trainer if an explanation is not clear or if they are lost. They are more likely to remain quiet and to hope that they will catch up. This situation will undoubtedly create a certain amount of panic for a trainee. Inattentiveness may result because a trainee in this situation is worrying about what has been missed rather than what the trainer is now covering.

It is important for trainers to establish a pace that is suitable to the material being covered as well as to the ability of the trainees to grasp the material. Otherwise, a great deal of time is wasted in retraining, and considerable frustration as well as other negative feelings will occur for the trainee.

2. *Minimizing the difficulty of learning.* Most trainers want to find a way to put trainees at ease and to reassure them that the material can be learned easily. Often this desire results in the trainer beginning instruc-

tion by saying, "This is simple and you shouldn't have any difficulty."
The reaction of the trainee, unfortunately, is not one of being made to
feel at ease but one of anxiety. What if trainees do have questions or have
not understood? Does their confusion mean they are incapable of performing the job? While it is important to reassure trainees about their
ability to grasp material, this particular approach will likely backfire if
used too often.

Instead, the trainer might begin by indicating that at first trainees
might find the procedure or equipment a little overwhelming because it is
new, but once they have learned the basics they should not find it difficult. The trainer might also explain that while trainees may have questions and possibly initial difficulties, the trainer is sure that they will be
successful once they have learned the basic operation. The trainer should
strive, therefore, to put the operation into the context of the *new* person,
not into context of an experienced person. Words of reassurance should
be such that they do not discourage questions or belittle the person, albeit
accidentally.

3. *Praise and correction.* Job training most often occurs in the work environment, not at some remote location. Training may occur at terminals,
at the card catalog, at the reference desk, or in the reception area of the
administrative office. Because trainees are instructed in locations where
other staff or the public are immediately adjacent, trainers need to be particularly sensitive to ways in which they can instruct and correct without
either intimidating or humiliating trainees. For instance, it will be difficult to provide instruction in filing in the card catalog without also pointing out mistakes at the same time. Even so, the trainer should be sensitive
in handling corrections or evaluation of performance when other staff—
or the public—can overhear. The general axiom of "praise in public, correct in private" should be the premise on which trainers interact with
trainees.

Whenever possible, training should be conducted first "behind the
scenes." For instance, rather than instructing someone in the basic rules
of filing in the public catalog at the catalog, the trainer could have a set of
"dummy" cards that could be used to provide initial training with the
necessary correction. Once the trainee has demonstrated a grasp of the
filing rules, he or she could be taken to the public catalog area to begin to
work with actual filing. The trainer should work next to the trainee and
be sensitive to the tone and volume of his or her voice when providing
further instruction and correction. In other situations where training
cannot occur except in the immediate work area, the trainer should talk
with the trainee beforehand to outline how they will approach the training and particularly the correcting of mistakes.

The issue of how to correct staff is one that should be given very careful consideration, because pointing out mistakes publicly has a negative impact on the person's self-esteem and sense of worth. This in turn affects the trainees' attitude toward all aspects of working for the library, even though the trainee's discouragement may not be immediately obvious to the trainer or the supervisor.

4. *Conflicting messages*. Trainers need to avoid sending conflicting messages to trainees. They need to be aware of the relationship between verbal and non-verbal behavior and to recognize that non-verbal behavior always carries the most powerful message between people. If trainees receive confusing and conflicting messages from trainers, particularly if such communication results in their own embarrassment, their reaction will be anger, discouragement, and low morale.

If a trainer indicates to trainees that it is acceptable to interrupt to ask questions, or to return as often as possible to ask questions, then their expectation will be that the trainer will respond positively. Instead, too often a trainee will get an exasperated response such as "You mean you didn't understand that?," or "This has been clear to everyone else," or "Could you go reread the manual first?" Now the trainee has been told one thing—ask questions—but has received a very different response upon asking questions—don't ask or, worse, bright staff don't need to ask! In this environment, trainees are going to be hurt and angry; they may well have negative feelings about their own abilities, and therefore they will likely not trust the trainer in the future. This situation is often made much worse when the comments are made in front of co-workers or the public.

Another typical example of conflicting messages being sent during training occurs when trainers or supervisors indicate that they believe staff "learn from mistakes." When actually practiced, this attitude by a supervisor can put employees at ease and can assure them that they can try new activities or tasks without fear of reprisals if a mistake is made. This attitude encourages staff to accept responsibility and to take initiative, and should increase the likelihood that staff will continue to contribute to the library. Unfortunately, this philosophy is not always followed in practice. When mistakes are made, the employee is "chewed out" and made to feel as though the mistake will certainly bring the department, if not the library, to a grinding halt. Responding to a mistake with comments such as "How could you possibly have done that? It's so easy to follow!," or "Well, this has made a lot of work for me now," or "Boy, is this going to make the boss mad!" will not correct the problem nor will it assist the trainee in learning from the mistake. If indeed the supervisor and trainer want trainees to learn from mistakes, supervisors should see

such occurrences as opportunities to analyze with the trainee what went
wrong and why. Trainers should use mistakes as a constructive way to
assist trainees to develop a better understanding of procedures, or to organize their work more effectively, or to communicate when difficulties
arise, and so forth. It is unlikely that any one mistake in a library will
create an irreversible problem; therefore, supervisors and trainers should
not overreact and make trainees feel as though they have jeopardized the
department or the library. If a mistake occurs that involves a library user,
then the supervisor can explain to the patron that a staff member still being trained had not fully understood a procedure and can do so without
humiliating the trainee. Indeed, when staff feel that they will not be pun-
ished for making mistakes, they often can and will identify their mistakes
and move to correct or resolve them. On the other hand, if they are pun-
ished for mistakes, then they will not be likely either to point them out
(which can create bigger problems) or make any effort to correct them.
While learning from mistakes is important, trainees should also understand the limits for repeating an error. The supervisor might indicate that
making a mistake once or even twice is considered part of the learning
process, but that making the same mistake repeatedly signals a learning
or performance problem.

Another conflicting message that trainees receive occasionally is that
they are told to seek assistance from co-workers when the trainer is not
available. When they pursue this approach and the trainer indicates dis-
pleasure by saying that ''Jim doesn't really have a grasp of the specific
task,'' then the trainee has been placed in a difficult position. In this case,
the trainee is again not going to trust the trainer and may in fact decide
that Jim is more pleasant to deal with and therefore accept his instructions and ignore those of the trainer. If the trainer does not want the
trainee to check with other staff, then this should be made clear. If other
staff should be used as resources, then the trainer should be clear about
which staff should be checked with on particular issues or problems, and
when.

The objective is to avoid confusing trainees while they are learning
and to avoid creating unnecessary tensions and distractions because of
conflicting messages being sent from the trainer to the trainee.

5. *Closed mind.* A trainer who believes that he or she knows everything
there is to know about a specific activity, task, or department will create
communication problems immediately. Trainers with this view of their
own knowledge will find it difficult to accept trainees' questioning and
differing views or ideas regarding procedures, policies, or people. Trainers who consider their own knowledge and opinions sufficient tend to react in a negative way when asked ''why,'' responding that ''We have

always done it this way" or "This is the best way." Closed-minded individuals do not usually like to provide explanations, since they believe that their view of the practice or procedure is a sufficient rationale. In other situations, staff with training responsibility may be unsure of their own abilities but not want to appear so to trainees. Thus, they react to questions in a negative manner, appearing to trainees as resistant to others' ideas or views.

Whatever the motivation for trainers, acting in this manner may create an environment in which few questions will be asked. Training may then evolve into a lecture process as the trainee retreats from active participation. Indeed, the trainee might learn early on to be reticent in trying new skills or in testing new ideas for fear of being judged too harshly by the trainer or supervisor.

Because of the critical role played by the trainer in the success of the learning process, these aspects of trainer style and approach should be carefully evaluated so that improvements can be made where needed.

Library Jargon. New employees joining an organization with which they have little or no familiarity must learn a new language. Every profession has its own jargon or terminology, and this jargon becomes a major barrier for the new person to overcome. The problem with language also occurs when certain changes are introduced, such as the installation of an automated system. Frequently, people working with automation use terminology with which few are familiar, and they often do not stop to explain meanings or usage. Terminology can become a problem even for library staff who move from one department to another, or in meetings that involve people from multiple departments. Library staff in one department can rely on specialized terminology and acronyms that are sometimes so esoteric that the original meanings escape even the most experienced library staff from another department. The heavy use of specialized language and acronyms makes library staff appear to be talking "in tongues" to those who are not familiar with the particular vocabulary. An example is the secretary in the administrative office of an academic research library who after two weeks asked in total frustration for someone to please explain ACRL, ALA, ARL, CLA, MLA, OCLC, . . . and the list went on; this individual had been struggling to make sense out of what to her was gibberish in order to function in her job. In another example, an individual joined the staff of a library that had a collective bargaining agreement and wondered why librarians spent so much time talking about the "union list"; she assumed, of course, that this referred to the list of union members.

One of the best ways to introduce new staff to library and department jargon is to prepare a brief glossary of the most frequently used terms or acronyms. A glossary can be reviewed during the first day so that the trainee can begin to grasp the definition and, more importantly, the use of the terms. Not all library terms can reasonably be put into a glossary. Therefore, the trainer and other staff need to be sensitive to explaining terms and usage. The trainer should ask periodically if there are any words that have not been explained or that are not clear, and the trainee should be encouraged to ask for explanations immediately when uncertain about a term. When a glossary does not exist, the trainee might be asked to keep a list of terms and acronyms with the definitions as they are given. This list would provide the trainee with a reference as he or she continues to learn library terms. In addition, what the trainee compiles could then be reviewed and edited by the supervisor and used for future trainees. This approach also involves the trainee immediately in contributing to the department by developing a useful tool for later use.

The communication issues that should be addressed during training are ones that require continual attention. When effective communication is used during training, it lays a positive foundation for future interactions.

Exercise

This exercise can be performed by the supervisor and trainer together or individually.

1. Consider mechanisms for feedback during training in your department. What needs improvement? Do you feel that you provide honest and constructive feedback on problems? Do you make time to praise staff performance? What difficulties exist, and what are reasonable goals for improving feedback during training?

2. Consider trainers' style, and identify the strengths of current trainers. Are those strengths being used in the best way? How can they be developed? Now consider trainers' weaknesses, and identify ways in which these can be minimized or eliminated.

3. Consider the extent to which jargon used in your department is (a) common to the library and (b) peculiar to your department.

Identify ways in which you can provide information to staff about terminology and usage, and minimize the negative impact of jargon.

Materials

Library training materials are often inadequate; either they do not exist, or what is used is poorly designed. Libraries have demonstrated the effective use of innovative teaching for instructing patrons in the use of library resources and bibliographic tools by developing self-instructional materials, slide-tape shows, and video presentations. Yet these same techniques have been used minimally for training and instructing library staff, even though their use would reduce costs and improve the effectiveness of training.

The formats and techniques that can be considered for use in developing training materials include audiovisual aids (slide-tape, filmstrip, video), computer-assisted instruction (particularly the use of microcomputers for simulation training), and written aids (programmed or self-instructional). The appropriate formats and techniques for training materials are determined by the subject or skills to be taught as well as the audience. Materials can be developed in segments or modules to allow brief and focused presentations and to provide trainees with the flexibility to review or learn a small portion of information at a time. For example, rather than developing a half-hour slide-tape show on the library's classification schemes, a more effective approach might be to develop individual contained segments on each classification system. The development of training materials in alternative formats should allow for an improvement in the quality of training. At the same time, it will free the supervisor or other staff from having to rely exclusively on time-consuming individual instruction.

Types of Materials. Materials are needed to support the orientation activity as well as skill and knowledge training. Supervisors need to identify materials that are required for new employees and those that are needed for current employees who will be working with new systems or new programs. The complexity of developing orientation materials is usually not as great as that required for developing training materials; but, nonetheless, to be effective in the orientation effort, quality materials are essential.

Orientation materials appropriate for new employees might include the following:

Brief description of the parent organization (objectives, organizational structure, size, activities, etc.) and its relationship to the library
Description of primary policies and benefits, and information on how to obtain more details

Library organization chart, and description of basic activities of library departments

Explanation of library mission and goals, policies, procedures, resources, services, and staff directory

Department organization chart, and description of objectives and basic activities, names and positions of staff, and location of materials and supplies.

It is often helpful to have an orientation checklist that supervisors can use as a reminder of the topics, issues, and information that should be covered during the orientation period.

Supervisors also need to consider what background information or materials would be appropriate for staff who will participate in a new project or new assignment. For instance, what descriptive general materials might be helpful to staff when implementing a database search service, or implementing an online circulation system, or altering the cataloging requirements. The purpose of orientation is to provide a work context and thus contribute to an employee's understanding of and commitment to the activities of the library. Therefore, it is important that orientation materials not focus soley on new employees, but that they recognize the needs of continuing staff as well.

Some libraries have put effort into developing more sophisticated orientation materials, such as slide-tape or video presentations explaining the library organization for new staff. Such materials can be very effective when well presented, because they not only provide information, they contribute to positive feelings about the library.

Other types of orientation materials are often available for library supervisors to use. The parent organization (such as the college, business, or special foundation) may have developed introductory materials to the organization for fundraising purposes, and these might be appropriate to show to new employees as well. Certain other materials may be available to provide staff orientation to specific equipment or systems. For instance, the local telephone company may have a film that could be borrowed by the library on the use of the phone system and phone courtesy. Vendors and utilities serving libraries may have materials that could be used to introduce staff to the system and services prior to the skills training.

Library supervisors should also determine whether materials produced for library users would be useful for staff in learning the library organization and in developing an appreciation for the range and scope of activities and services.

Instructional materials are even more critical to effective training and therefore demand attention from supervisors. As library operations become more complex, particularly with the expansion of automated systems, the difficulties faced in training with nonexistent or inadequate materials only confound the problem of implementing change.

The process of developing training materials is difficult, and a considerable level of skill to produce quality materials is required. Supervisors should begin by acknowledging that a manual is not an instructional or training material; at best, it is a source document. Too often in libraries, trainees are given an operations or department manual to read. If the trainees have no opportunity to apply what they read, they are unlikely to retain the information and may indeed be confused by a great deal of what is contained in the manual. Instead, a trainer can use sections of a manual as he or she trains for a specific function or task so that trainees know that there is a source to go back to in order to check details once instruction is concluded.

Supervisors should recognize the problems that exist with the use of manuals, particularly with the use of outdated manuals. The training process can be seriously impeded if trainees are instructed to read a manual that is partially outdated or inaccurate. If trainees are aware that the manual is inaccurate, they will not be inclined to put much energy into the activity, will see it as a futile exercise, and will wonder why the supervisor wants them to waste time. All of these concerns could result in the trainees' losing respect for the supervisor and trust in the accuracy of future materials given during the training process. Therefore, outdated sections should be deleted or clearly marked. Again, manuals should not be seen as instructional materials but as sources that can be referred to during training.

Training materials should *complement* personal instruction but should not replace it entirely. Personal interaction is needed to clarify, to test knowledge and ability, and to support and encourage.

The following criteria should be considered in developing materials for skills training: (1) materials should be designed to provide information about a single knowledge area or task at a time, (2) trainees should be able to use materials independently or as part of training sessions, and (3) trainees should have a means for self-testing so that they will know if the information has been absorbed or the skill has been acquired.

In addition to using training materials developed by library staff, materials developed by other sources should be identified and reviewed for use. Materials developed by other libraries, library associations, utilities or vendors, and commercial producers should all be investigated. It is a good idea to preview materials with staff before purchasing or using them on a regular basis so that the materials are appropriate and likely to contribute to training results.

One final comment about training materials: library professionals need to begin to exert more pressure and demands on vendors of automated systems to improve the quality of the materials they provide with their systems. Specifically, vendors should be expected to develop well-written and comprehensive training materials that library supervisors will be able to use in the implementation of an automated system. This request should be part of the process of negotiating a contract with a vendor. Unless library professionals are willing to make more demands in this area, they will continue to have to absorb all of the requirements for developing and testing training materials for these systems.

Exercise

This exercise can be done by the supervisor and trainer together or individually. It is one in which it would be useful to involve other department staff.

1. List the orientation materials that are provided to the new employee by the parent institution, by the library, and by the department. What other materials should be included? How can you acquire these additional materials? If someone in your department has to prepare material, such as a glossary, who would be qualified to do this?

2. List the training materials that are available in your department and what functions or activities they serve. What other training materials would be a high priority to develop or acquire? Who would be qualified to develop training materials in your department?

3. Finally, what training materials are currently being used in the department that are outdated or inappropriate, such as manuals? What actions must be taken to update materials or to eliminate the use of inappropriate materials?

Scheduling Training

The final consideration in implementing training is setting the actual schedule for the date, time, and location of the training activities. The supervisor and trainer should have already identified the order for training segments; but immediately before training begins, a specific schedule should be developed. Scheduling should not be done too far in advance in order to avoid having to make numerous changes in the schedule because of other intervening time demands on the trainer or equipment. Two primary considerations should be reviewed when establishing a schedule: departmental needs and the needs of the trainee.

Departmental and Trainer Considerations. In considering departmental requirements, the supervisor should be concerned with minimizing disruptions to normal work flow, the availability of resources such as equipment, and the schedule of or demands placed on the trainer. Most library training occurs in the immediate workplace, and thus the likelihood of some disruptions to other staff or to the public must be considered. The supervisor needs to consider what the best time for training will be so that other staff's work or the ability of the public to use library facilities is not seriously disrupted. For instance, if the supervisor knows that patrons use the public catalog most heavily starting at about 11:00 A.M., then scheduling training for new filers during this same time period would not be wise.

In planning training for an online system, the supervisor should consider the off-peak time and the least expensive time to use the system. Based on this information, a schedule can be set up that takes advantage of the availability of the equipment in relation to production work and costs. Too often, training just happens without reference to how the schedule affects the department.

The trainer's time and attention are other considerations in determining the best schedule for training. The trainer should be able to give full attention to the training activity and not be diverted with reference questions from patrons or interruptions from other staff.

Trainee Needs. Another component to consider when scheduling training is the needs of the trainee. If several employees are to be trained at one time, it becomes more difficult to consider their individual needs. Some review of the trainee's needs, however, is worthwhile in order to maximize the training effort. In particular, a supervisor might consider the following: normal attention span in relation to a particular subject or activity, and the energy levels of individual trainees. With a highly technical subject, a trainee's attention is likely to wander after thirty or forty minutes because of difficulty in absorbing too much material. Most people know whether they are more alert and attentive in the morning or in the afternoon. The idea is to schedule training in such a way as not to exceed a normal attention span for the subject matter and, when possible, to capitalize on the individual's high energy periods for particularly difficult instruction.

While a supervisor may not always have sufficient flexibility to take all of these factors into account (particularly individual trainee needs), they are worth considering. The supervisor primarily needs to build variety into the training process to avoid overload and boredom. If the trainees are lectured at for several hours, their attention may drift, and their ability to translate the information into action will be low. Trainees need a mixture of lecture, presentation or demonstration, observation, practice, and reading. This mixture will not only be more likely to keep their attention at a peak level, but it will provide trainees with a number of ways both to learn and to test what they have learned. Using a variety of approaches makes the training more interesting and sets a reasonable pace for the person. It is difficult to sustain attention and interest if trainees are asked to absorb a lecture on a very complex procedure or routine late in the day. Although supervisors will not always be able to tailor the training scheduling to fit all of the needs of individual trainees, they should at least review the needs of the people to be trained as part of the scheduling activity.

By combining both the departmental and trainee needs, the supervisor should arrive at a balance that will be likely to increase the results from the training effort.

Exercise

This exercise can be conducted by the supervisor and trainer together or individually.

1. Consider the way in which training has been scheduled for departmental trainees in the past, and identify what problems may have occurred with disruptions to operations and with the trainees. Have there been any difficulties in getting access to materials or equipment for the training function?

2. What steps can be taken to improve the training schedule in relation to departmental and trainer needs?

5

EVALUATION OF TRAINING

The final planning component in job training is evaluation. Although this segment is presented as a separate chapter, the actual activity of planning for evaluation should occur when training objectives and content are being established. The process and purpose of evaluating job training are similar to other evaluative responsibilities of a supervisor: to gather and analyze information in order to justify past actions, and to project the future use of departmental resources—staff and materials. When job training has been treated informally, the evaluation of this function has also been informal or nonexistent. Once a supervisor invests significant time and energy into improving the job training activity, an informal approach to evaluation diminishes the potential for future effectiveness and efficiency. The evaluation step allows the supervisor to seek improvements in training while building on the strengths that exist.

Conroy suggests that the following goals can be achieved through the evaluation of training:

> Furnish accurate information to assist further planning, to improve decision-making, and to document achievements
> Determine to what extent a program and/or activity is accomplishing its goals and objectives, and what results are being achieved.
> Identify program strengths and weaknesses and the reasons for specific successes and failures
> Assure more consistent quality in learning activities and efforts
> Reinforce learning and develop an awareness of growth and change
> Determine the cost and benefits of the program and its activities
> Justify the investment and answer demands for accountability

Produce documentation that allows information to be shared with others.[1]

Though Conroy is focusing on the evaluation of organization-wide training efforts, these points have validity for evaluating departmental job training efforts as well. This list can serve as a set of broad objectives for the evaluation of job training.

While it is true that all job training should be evaluated, there will need to be differences in approach to evaluation and methodology based on the position for which the job training is provided. The methodology and amount of effort devoted to the evaluation of job training will vary for different training situations. Certain positions require more extensive training in depth, scope, and length of training time, and these training efforts should receive more thorough attention in the evaluation of the training. In other situations, large numbers of staff may be trained at one time for the same task or operation, and this will require modification in the approach to evaluation. Supervisors will therefore need to make adjustments in approaches for both training and evaluation of training not because some positions are worth less or more than others, but because of the nature of the positions and the training context.

For instance, the evaluation of job training for a large number of hourly employees at the beginning of a semester in a college library would be structured somewhat differently than for a single clerical or professional position. In the former situation, the supervisor might decide to evaluate training by using a simple questionnaire to obtain feedback from the student employees, or to evaluate training on a semester basis when most new student assistants are hired. In establishing mechanisms for obtaining feedback about the training a person in a supervisory position receives, the manager may determine that meetings to assess progress in training will be held less often than for other positions, because more time is needed to acquire the necessary knowledge and skill for a supervisory position.

In every situation, the supervisor planning the training will need to make decisions regarding appropriate methods for evaluation within the context of the training. The following sections provide suggestions on methods for approaching the evaluation of the job training activity.

1. Barbara Conroy, *Library Staff Development and Continuing Education* (Littleton, Colo.: Libraries Unlimited, 1978), p.191.

Who Evaluates

The first question to be addressed for evaluation is who will have responsibility for actually evaluating the job training. Several staff usually participate in job training activities; these same people should have a role in the evaluation as well. Specifically, the supervisor, the trainer(s) and the trainee(s) all have a role in evaluating the job training activity. In some situations, it might be appropriate to have a third-party evaluation, such as by co-workers who either know specifics of the job well and can comment on training or who interact with some aspect of the trainee's performance.

Everyone who is involved in the evaluation of job training should share a common goal to determine if the training "worked." Did the trainee learn what was taught? Can the trainee perform job duties and tasks as required? Each individual evaluating the job training will be influenced by his or her own role and position in relation to the training activity, and this bias must be weighed by the supervisor when analyzing the information provided by those who are doing the evaluating.

The supervisor has the responsibility for outlining how the evaluation will be accomplished and for analyzing the information in order to make future decisions. In addition, through observation and discussions with the staff involved in the training process, the supervisor will be in a position to evaluate results from his or her perspective. The supervisor has to be concerned with both effectiveness (quality) and efficiency (cost) in evaluating training. The supervisor will focus on the specifics of the training, as well as on the overall impact of training on departmental performance—work flow, services, and relationships among staff.

The trainee will be most concerned with whether everything that will be required in knowledge and skill has been presented and learned before independent performance is expected. The trainee will be very attuned to the learning environment, relationships with co-workers and the trainer. Finally, the trainee can evaluate the schedule and pace of training in relation to his or her own abilities.

The perspective of the trainer is whether the end result of the training has been achieved. Indeed, the trainer focuses on whether success has been achieved with the trainee and therefore if the training process is concluded. The trainer is also likely to be concerned with his or her own performance in the training process.

Though there will be overlap among the people who evaluate training, their different perspectives contribute a greater scope and depth to the evaluation process.

What to Evaluate

There are two broad objectives in evaluation of job training: (1) an assessment of the trainee's performance as a result of training and (2) the effectiveness and efficiency of the training. It will not be sufficient to focus only on the performance of the trainee without considering whether the desired performance is a result of the training itself. At the same time, there has to be a consideration of whether the training was conducted in the most efficient manner in using staff time, materials, and equipment.

The best evaluation results will occur if performance objectives have been clearly stated as part of the training plan. As each segment of the training plan is being developed, the supervisor should ask "What should the trainee have learned?" and "What do we want to result from the training?" By focusing on evaluation as part of the initial planning process, the supervisor will ensure that the evaluation is integrated into the overall training plan and also that the objectives and content of training are appropriate to meet job and departmental needs.

Kearsley describes the points that evaluation should cover in the following way:

> Improved efficiency—same results with fewer costs.
> Improved effectiveness—better results with same costs.
> Improved productivity—better results with lower costs. [2]

In order to conduct training evaluation to meet these broad categories, specific information on the following topics needs to be gathered:

> Trainee performance
> Trainee reaction to the training
> Training process, content, and learning environment
> Trainer strengths and weaknesses
> Costs (staff, materials, and equipment).

Trainee Performance. Certainly, the most obvious place to focus evaluation is on the performance of the trainee and on the desired change in behavior. Is the trainee able to perform tasks and activities at the level of expectation? Does the trainee exhibit the preferred behavior and attitudes? Since job training should be evaluated throughout the training process, there will need to be "benchmarks" for performance as the trainee acquires knowledge and skill. These benchmarks should be articulated as

---

2. Greg Kearsley, *Cost, Benefits and Productivity in Training Systems* (Reading, Mass.: Addison-Wesley, 1982), p.3.

part of the training objectives. For example, database searching may have multiple criteria for performance evaluation, and these would be applied differentially to a reference librarian as he or she moved through the training process. The criteria might include the ability to apply search strategies, knowledge of descriptors, formulation time, interview time, search costs and number of searches that are rerun, and degree to which the search is handled independently. If training objectives have been defined against these performance criteria or expectations, then evaluation of the training will be straightforward.

Since individual trainees bring different skills and experiences to the training situation for a particular job, these should be taken into account when evaluating the results of training. If these differences are overlooked, the supervisor might view the training process as achieving the desired results when actually the performance was based on the trainee's previous knowledge and ability.

Training Process, Content, and Learning Environment. Evaluation of training should include more than just the evaluation of the trainee's performance. It is important to evaluate specific aspects of the training, not just the end product. By doing so, the supervisor can be more certain of what is successful and what needs improvement. The process, content, and learning environment should be evaluated, with the trainee being a key person to provide this evaluation; thus, the trainee's reaction to training is obtained. The trainee should be able to comment on whether the content was appropriate (was more or less needed), whether it was provided in a clear manner, whether the relationship among the topics was logical for the purpose of learning, whether the schedule was reasonable, and whether a sufficient variety of activities was presented. Did the trainee feel that there was adequate support and direction from the trainer and co-workers during the training process? Were questions encouraged and answered fully and in a constructive manner? In addition, the trainee can be asked whether communication with the supervisor was adequate and timely. Finally, the trainee can be asked what might be done to improve the training process. The trainee might be asked to suggest whether anything was overlooked or given insufficient attention during training, or what materials might have been useful, such as a glossary.

The purpose of evaluation is to assess the overall process of training as well as the specific modules and units within the training plan. The supervisor wants to focus on the total outcome, particularly keeping in mind the need to address issues of motivation, job satisfaction, commitment, and loyalty that should be developed as part of the training process.

Trainer Strengths and Weaknesses. In order to support successful training efforts in a department, the supervisor will need feedback on the trainer(s). When this information is sought from the trainee, it should be handled carefully in order not to create tensions between the trainer and the trainee. Indeed, new employees are likely to be reluctant to be candid in this regard for fear of alienating co-workers. The supervisor should find a way to acquire information from the trainee in a manner that does not threaten the trainee or embarrass the trainer. The trainee can provide feedback on the trainer's instructional style, the clarity of his or her communication, and the support and guidance the trainer provided.

The trainer also has a valuable role in evaluating his or her own performance as a trainer. This role is particularly important if the trainer's responsibility is a new one. Indeed, all trainers should be expected to evaluate all aspects of the training in which they are involved: the process, content, schedule, pace, and the individual trainee's abilities, as well as the trainer's own abilities. If the supervisor presents the evaluation process as a means of strengthening the training activity, then the trainer will likely be open to assessing his or her own performance and accepting suggestions for improvement.

Finally, the supervisor has a responsibility to assess the trainer's performance through observation.

Cost. It is necessary to identify all of the various costs related to the designing, implementing, and monitoring of the job training. An improvement in the efficiency of training is another motivating reason to improve library training activities. While the employee is still being trained, he or she is not a fully contributing member of the organization; indeed, the person is a drain on the organization's resources as other staff train him or her. Thus, the supervisor should evaluate the training effort in order to determine whether job training is as efficient as it might be. In this regard, costs should be determined for the following:

Staff resources to:

develop a training plan
organize and prepare related materials, such as manuals and handouts
design workbooks and instructional materials
conduct training (trainer and trainee time)
retrain (trainer and trainee time)
evaluate training.

Materials and equipment:

written materials (paper, printing, or photocopying)
audio-visual materials (purchase, rental, or production)
telecommunication time
equipment rental.

There has not been much attempt in libraries to assess the costs for training. In addition, there is no information available on costs of inadequate training—costs in wasted time, error rates, and higher equipment or telecommunications rates (such as for database searching, online cataloging, etc.). At the very least, supervisors should begin to assess costs related to training. This assessment provides them with the information needed to determine where improvements should be made to reduce costs or to realize increased quality for the dollars already expended on training. Tracking costs should not be viewed as a way to reduce the commitment to training; instead, it should be seen as a necessary element in strengthening training.

When and How to Evaluate

The process of evaluation should be integrated into the training plan, not be performed as a separate activity that is grafted on at some point after training is completed. In addition, the evaluation process will be most effective if it is approached in a number of different ways and conducted both formally and informally. The following section suggests different points at which evaluation might occur and mechanisms for evaluation.

Before Training Starts. Supervisors need to assess the level and extent of a staff member's abilities in relation to the requirements of the job. In some environments, this may involve a pre-test in order to determine specific knowledge that the individual possesses. In most cases, though, assessment is more informal. For a new employee, the supervisor has information obtained through the interview and reference process. This information can be supplemented with a discussion regarding job requirements and the training plan on the very first day of employment in order to check assumptions about the person's knowledge and skill.

Information about current staff should be available through past performance evaluations, observations, and discussions, and this information provides the basis for assessing where the staff member might begin

in the training process. With new staff, though, it may be worthwhile to
ask an individual before training begins to assess his or her strengths and
weaknesses in relation to the planned training.

The point to remember is that some mechanism should be used to determine the abilities of staff before beginning a training process so that
the plan can be modified where appropriate.

Is this step really evaluation? Yes, because the supervisor needs to
evaluate completely the point at which the trainee is beginning in order to
evaluate the success of the training process. If a trainee lacks an ability
that the supervisor assumes exists, then the trainee will have difficulty
during training. Equally true, if trainees are more experienced than has
been anticipated, they may become bored and impatient with the training. Therefore, the supervisor needs to evaluate the base line of knowledge, skills, and abilities trainees possess before the training begins.

During Training. Job training should be flexible enough to be modified
and adjusted as the training is occurring. In order to achieve flexibility,
information will need to be available to the supervisor and to the trainer
throughout the process, not just at the conclusion of training. One of the
most effective ways to monitor training is for review meetings to be established throughout the training period. When training a *new* employee, it
is suggested that review meetings be held weekly during the first four to
eight weeks of employment, depending on the complexity and length of
the training process. A weekly review meeting should be held between the
trainer and the trainee, between the trainee and the supervisor, and between the supervisor and the trainer. This approach can be modified, of
course, depending on the level of the position. For instance, with tempo-
rary or hourly employees, such as student assistants, it is probably not
reasonable to hold such frequent review sessions, particularly if their
training is very task specific and completed in a short time frame. On the
other hand, for an individual filling a department head position, bi-
weekly meetings might be sufficient. The intent here is to suggest a guideline that can be modified to suit the particular situation, taking into account the experience of the person being trained and the complexity of
the position and of the environment.

Review meetings between *trainer and trainee* are suggested when there is
a primary trainer rather than a number of staff training in very specific
tasks or duties. The focus of this review should be on what has been
learned, where problems occurred and why, what may need to be repeated, and whether the training can be accelerated. Further, the trainer
and trainee should discuss the pace and mix of training activities, as well
as whether communication in instruction is clear. The trainer should

provide the trainee with an overall assessment of his or her progress, as well as with comments on what was accomplished within each segment of the week's training. This assessment should be honest so that the trainee does not assume that progress is being made when it is not. If the trainee is not informed about problems early on, then correction will be impossible, and such problems are usually compounded as the training progresses. In these review meetings, both the trainer and the trainee benefit from a frank discussion regarding the entire training for that week. Also, at this weekly meeting, the trainer and trainee review the plans for the next week of training.

The supervisor needs an update from the trainer on the progress of the trainee, on any problems encountered that disrupted training, and on plans for the next week. A meeting between trainer and supervisor is an opportunity for the supervisor to determine whether the trainee is progressing within the objectives of the training plan and, if not, to determine what corrective action might be taken. Secondly, it is an opportunity for the supervisor to assess how the trainer is handling the training responsibilities and to provide support and direction. Finally, the supervisor must assert his or her continued interest in and responsibility for all staff even though the training is being conducted by someone else.

A review meeting between supervisor and trainee provides a chance for the supervisor to interact directly with the trainee to determine this person's view of the training process and his or her progress. This meeting allows the supervisor to continue to establish a presence with the staff in the vital area of training and to determine if values and expectations are being adequately represented. This meeting with the supervisor also allows the trainee to express any difficulties or frustrations with the training process including with the trainer. While it is unlikely that a new employee is going to be very forthright in criticizing an experienced staff member, this meeting at least provides an opportunity for the supervisor and staff member to talk.

There will be some situations in which other library staff should be asked to contribute to the evaluation of training. For instance, some reference departments use an evaluation process that involves the librarians in evaluating one another using specific criteria. Young reports that at the University of Arizona Library's Central Reference Department, a checklist representing reference standards and behaviors within these standards was developed to provide an evaluation tool.[3] He describes the five major reference skills that are included in this checklist: communica-

3. William F. Young, "Methods for Evaluating Reference Desk Service," *RQ* 25 (Fall 1985):72.

tion style (verbal and non-verbal) with users, user interaction at the reference desk, co-worker interaction at the reference desk, knowledge of collections, and personal qualities or traits exhibited at the desk toward
co-workers and users. Within each of these reference standards are desired behaviors that form the basis of evaluation. This method of evaluation could be used for the reference librarian during the training process
as well to allow colleagues at the desk the opportunity to provide feedback
to the supervisor. Young also describes a similar system at the State University of New York at Oswego, Penfield Library. Schwartz and Eakin
similarly describe a colleague evaluation process at the Taubman Medical Library, University of Michigan.[4] A set of standards for performance
at the reference desk have been developed. Periodically, the reference librarians are asked to complete a checklist of reference skills for their colleagues, evaluating performance in the categories of attitude and de-
meanor; interviewing, listening, and referring; search strategy;
knowledge of resources and collections; and knowledge of services and
policies. These examples indicate that there are situations in which evaluation or review by colleagues may be appropriate, and this review process
can be used equally effectively during training as well as for continuing
performance evaluation. The trainee should always be aware when this
approach will be used and understand the process and the basis of the
evaluation. During the training process, a variety of checks or tests are
conducted to monitor the trainee's progress. In some jobs, revision is
done to correct mistakes and to identify further training needs. Oftentimes, a trainee is asked to demonstrate a particular task or is observed
when performing some aspect of the job assignment. For instance, stacks
supervisors may tag books in order to determine accuracy of shelving by
new shelvers. The concept of checking specific tasks or activities is not
unusual in libraries. It should be recognized that this traditional process
of checking performance is also a way to evaluate training. What needs to
be added to this task approach for checking or revising work is a review of
the trainee's overall progress and performance in relation to the training
plan.

Conclusion of Training. A mechanism for evaluating the results of training
at the end of the process should be established. This mechanism might
involve several components, such as a final review meeting similar to the
periodic meetings, a questionnaire for the trainee to complete to evaluate
the entire training process, or a "quiz" for the trainee to test some spe-

---

4. Diane G. Schwartz and Dottie Eakin, "Reference Service Standards, Performance
Criteria, and Evaluation," *Journal of Academic Librarianship* 12 (March 1986):4–8.

cific aspects of knowledge and skills. What is important is to wrap up the training by evaluating results and not simply allow it to trail off into the dust. This review is also important so that the trainee recognizes that the formal training, at least, is completed.

At this time, it should also be clear whether follow-up evaluation of performance related to what was provided during training will be conducted. A review should also be considered at some point after the trainee is working independently to determine if the training "took" and whether the person can indeed perform all of the job activities at the level of defined expectations or standards. When this final review is planned, it should be stated as part of the training plan.

Analyzing Evaluation Information

As was indicated earlier, the supervisor will be making decisions regarding the training as evaluation is conducted throughout the training process. At the completion of the formal training process, the supervisor should then consider all of the information obtained and determine what future changes might be made in the training process, such as the content, approach, pace, and trainers. The supervisor will need to sort out what was specifically related to a particular trainee or to a situation within the department that is unlikely to reoccur, and what occurred that suggests that permanent modifications are needed. As evaluation information is collected over a period of time, the supervisor will be able to assess trends and be able to obtain an overview of specific and general aspects of job training.

The supervisor can use the evaluation data to identify future training needs for trainers, the need for improved training materials, and possible ways to reduce staff costs related to training. As the supervisor considers the responses to departmental training, he or she may gain insights into other aspects of the department that might be improved, such as communication and cooperation among staff. The supervisor might also gain information related to high turnover or continuing performance problems. Finally, the supervisor may develop ideas on how to continue to prepare the departmental staff for future changes in work routines, work flow, job assignments, and skill requirements. In general, job training evaluation is another important source of information to assist the supervisor in considering ways to improve the use of the most valuable resources—the staff.

Exercise

This exercise can be conducted by the supervisor and the trainer together or working alone.

1. Review each segment of the training plan and determine the method(s) for the evaluation of trainee performance and progress. How will these evaluation points be described and conducted?

2. Determine the methods for acquiring feedback from the trainee on his or her views and suggestions about the training.

3. Describe your expectations for trainer performance, and develop standards to evaluate effectiveness.

4. Identify the costs that you will monitor, and describe how this monitoring will be accomplished.

5. What follow-up will be done on training after it has been completed, when, and how?

6

BEYOND THE TRAINING PLAN

Libraries, as information service organizations, have a large proportion of jobs that fall into the category defined by Drucker as "knowledge work."[1] Drucker indicates that managing the knowledge worker will be the challenge of tomorrow. Difficulties in managing lie in trying to define productivity and accomplishments for knowledge workers, since the results of their work are not always observable or at least not for some time. Library staff are highly representative of knowledge workers, consisting as they do of supervisors, managers, reference librarians, selectors, and catalogers—hereafter referred to as professional staff. These professional positions involve the coordination of human resources, and the organization of and provision of information, all of which are responsibilities involving a range of intellectual activities.

The knowledge work environment with all of its attendant complexities also requires greater demands in training staff that fill these positions. Therefore, supervisors need to go beyond the training plan to identify multiple approaches for staff learning and development. A longer time span (one to three years) will be required both to train staff and to measure results from training efforts. This is not to suggest that a training plan is not in fact useful for all library positions at all levels of the organization but that more may be required for many library positions.

Several options that can be used to extend the more standard job training include coaching, role modeling, goal setting, and the use of outside training and development resources. As the supervisor develops a train-

---

1. Peter F. Drucker, *Management: Tasks, Responsibilities, Practices* (New York: Harper & Row, 1973), p.176.

ing plan for professional positions, these options should be recognized as legitimate avenues for staff development.

Coaching and Role Modeling

Two of the most important vehicles for training and development are the coaching and role modeling that an experienced supervisor or colleague can provide to a more junior person. While coaching and role modeling cannot be structured into a training plan, they are still valuable as means to train and should be recognized as such.

Coaching is the responsibility that a supervisor has to provide ongoing direction, support, and correction to staff. It goes beyond merely correcting mistakes, and instead focuses on assisting the person to see opportunities, consider alternatives, and develop strategies. Coaching should focus on the individual in a broad sense: the person's needs for growth and development beyond a specific position. Coaching suggests to the junior individual that the supervisor has a commitment to his or her success and learning. Supervisors who coach staff recognize that their experience and perspective are a valuable resource to other staff, and they share their expertise willingly. Further, coaching is not always provided solely by the immediate supervisor, nor should it be. Supervisors should encourage professional staff to accept coaching from other members of the library staff or in the profession, because one can benefit from a broad spectrum of views and opinions.

While the amount of coaching cannot be prescribed and will vary based on the individuals involved, supervisors should be alert to the opportunities that this informal approach to training allows. It can be a far less threatening and more relaxed environment in which to discuss particularly sensitive issues of personal development.

Role modeling is another way that staff learn, although it is subtle and often not recognized at all as part of training. A manager of a department or division needs to recognize that his or her approach to supervision sets the example for those supervisors and staff who report to him or her. The alert manager recognizes that ''actions speak louder than words'' and that no matter what philosophy is espoused, supervisors under him or her are more likely to believe and emulate behavior not philosophy. Thus, when a manager describes expectations for communication, participation, and staff development, the supervisor will naturally (though not necessarily consciously) look to the manager as an example. Therefore, much of what the manager wants the supervisor to learn must be set by example as well as by directive. If a manager indicates that performance evaluation is important to the health of the organization and that time and effort should be devoted to it, then the supervisor will rightly expect support and recognition for this effort. If support is not forthcoming, and indeed if the manager provides little to the supervisor in the way of a performance evaluation, the supervisor will "learn" that this activity is not a priority after all and respond accordingly with his or her own staff.

Acting as a role model occurs because of the seniority of one's position and experience not because of choice. The recognition of this fact may offer opportunities for the supervisor that may not have been tapped previously. The supervisor can look for situations in which a person's participation or observation might provide a learning experience, and also be sensitive to how his or her own behavior is providing indicators of priorities and acceptable behavior.

Goal Setting

Another method for training and developing professional staff is through goal setting. Establishing performance goals provides a future-oriented and result-oriented basis of communication between the manager and the professional. Although the supervisor defines the initial performance goals when developing the training plan, these goals will have to be revised and updated as the person becomes more capable and confident in the position, and as department priorities change. Through the process of focusing on the performance results that are wanted, the supervisor is assisting the professional in identifying gaps in knowledge, skill, and ability and in finding ways to close the gaps. This process also allows the supervisor and staff member to identify new activities that might be undertaken and new skills that might be acquired. The focus should be on the growth and development of the individual, which in turn benefits the organization.

Goal setting, when used in a constructive way, should encourage personal development. If unrealistic goals are set, the process can be frustrating to the individual; or if punishment results from setting high goals that are not achieved, the individual may be discouraged and in the future show little initiative or willingness to take a risk.

More often, though, goal setting provides a comfortable format for ongoing communication between the supervisor and the professional; it is this dialogue and discussion that is most valuable. The actual writing of goals is simply a tool that provides the context for constructive discussion.

To be useful, goals need to be reviewed and updated at least twice a year. This interaction can provide the opportunity for planning, clarification, and development for the professional.

Other Training Sources

While supervisors have the primary responsibility for training and developing staff, not all training can occur within the department, particularly for professional positions that require a broad range of knowledge, skills, and abilities. Although staff filling these positions will often bring to the job many of the competencies required, they will need to enhance, refine, alter, or expand these skills as they adapt to a new environment or to changes within that environment. Primary sources for professional development include participation on library committees and in system-wide meetings, participation in workshops, and attendance at conferences.

Library Committees and Meetings. Professional staff should be encouraged to be actively involved in a variety of committee activities or meetings that allow for participation in projects outside of their specific job assignments. Staff learn from these opportunities by acquiring information, as well as by exposure to the perspectives and opinions of other staff. Committees tend to foster cooperation and the development of skills in deliberation, negotiation, and compromise. Committee responsibilities can also foster a recognition of the role of leadership (as differentiated from management) and the development of leadership skills.

Other library meetings can be used as a means to provide staff with the chance to discuss questions or problems, and to share ideas and experiences. For instance, periodic meetings among supervisory staff of a library would provide an opportunity for this group of staff to discuss specific topics (such as delegating responsibilities, controlling absenteeism, and conducting performance evaluations) and to draw on the ideas and viewpoints of one another. In a large library system, for example, reference librarians from the various divisions might benefit from periodic meetings to exchange ideas on bibliographic instruction and database searching.

In addition to holding job focused meetings, the library can encourage the professional staff to meet periodically to discuss broader topics, issues, or trends that are likely to affect the library or the profession. In many libraries, the professional staff meet periodically to discuss professional conferences they attended or research projects they are conducting. While it is difficult to measure the relationship of such meetings to improved job performance, they do provide opportunities from which potential learning and development may occur. These types of meetings do not have to be organized by the library administration, although the administration should encourage and support such meetings as a recognized means of continuing learning among professional staff and creating organizational cohesiveness.

Workshops. Increasingly, supervisors are looking to formal workshops offered by various associations and agencies to complement departmental training. In many cases, these workshops are needed to provide both basic and advanced training for supervisory and other professional staff because of the complexity and variety of knowledge, skills, and abilities needed by these individuals.

Depending on the size of the library and on the expertise that exists in specific areas, internal staff may be able to provide workshops on a range of subjects. When funds are available, trainers may be brought to the library to conduct workshops. It is also possible that several smaller libraries in a region could organize together to offer a workshop for their combined staffs. Library managers can also draw on other resources to supplement job training, such as library schools that offer workshops on professional or managerial topics; library associations—local, regional, and national; and commercial organizations. The use of these resources can be integrated into a job training plan when the supervisor knows about scheduled workshops, or topics can be identified for long-range development as opportunities occur.

Library supervisors should be alert to training opportunities that exist outside of the job setting and that support identified performance goals and department and library objectives. It is necessary, however, to be critical in assessing workshops in order to judge the appropriateness and the quality of programs. Supervisors should guard against the staff's viewing attendance at a workshop as a reward; this attitude does not contribute to a climate for learning or a commitment to a change in performance. To establish a mechanism for determining what workshops would be potentially useful, criteria should be developed against which supervisors and staff can judge the potential value of any workshop. The criteria might include the following questions:

> What is the specific content of the session, and how does it relate to the current and future needs and demands of the job, department, or library?

What are the goals for the person who will attend? What will the person be expected to do differently as a result of attendance at the workshop?

What changes or resources will be required to support the implementation of what the person learns?

These and other questions allow the supervisor and the professional to determine the relevance and timeliness of the workshop in relation to the needs of the library, and they ensure a greater likelihood of transferring what is learned from the workshop to the job setting.

There is also a need for supervisors and staff to evaluate the quality of the organization or person presenting the workshop. Some guidelines that might be brought to the evaluation include the following:

Background, experience, and reputation of workshop leaders.

The format of the workshop. Is variety offered in the workshop, such as lecture, discussion, case studies, role play, and films?

Who is the target audience, and how many participants will there be?

What do evaluations from previous workshops (if available) indicate about the quality of the program?

Finally, costs should be weighed, including the fee for the workshop, the time spent by the person attending the workshop, and related costs such as transportation, meals, and hotel, if applicable.

Once it has been determined that a staff member would benefit from participation in a workshop, then the supervisor needs to consider how he or she will reinforce the learning opportunity once the person returns from the workshop. Shortly after the workshop is concluded, the supervisor and staff member should meet to discuss the workshop and determine what steps the person will now take to implement what has been learned. The supervisor should encourage the individual to use the newly acquired knowledge and skills, and provide positive rewards when the person is successful.

Supervisors can make good use of training opportunities outside of the work setting while not losing the ability to influence how the newly acquired knowledge and skills will be used on the job. Supervisors who actively involve themselves in identifying results obtained from outside training programs also continue to play an active role in the development of staff even though they do not directly provide the learning experience.

Conferences. Attendance at conferences and participation in professional association activities add valuable dimensions to the professional's development. While libraries differ in the funding available to support staff attendance at conferences, they all can provide the time for such attendance.

Attending conferences provides the professional with a broader view of the library profession, establishes valuable contacts with colleagues from other organizations, and contributes to a pride in librarianship. The experienced professionals in a library should take responsibility for assisting the new professionals with learning the ropes in regard to professional association activities. Librarians also should consider the value of participating in professional associations in other fields that relate to their library responsibilities. For instance, the academic librarian may benefit from attendance at the Modern Language Association or the American Historical Association conferences. Librarians who work in a media center may benefit from participation at a conference that focuses on new technology and software.

Although it may be more difficult to "measure" the effectiveness of participation in professional conference in relation to job responsibilities, it is reasonable to expect that librarians who actively engage in conference activities will gain knowledge that will be useful to the library.

In reviewing these other avenues for training and development for library professional positions, it is obvious that the time frame for professional development will be much greater than for clerical development, and greater creativity will be required. Supervisors have a responsibility to recognize where different needs exist in staff training and to plan accordingly.

Training in the Electronic Library

As libraries become increasingly automated, will staff training have to alter? Will there be new requirements and considerations for training? Will training be more demanding and difficult for supervisors? The answer to all of these is a resounding *yes*.

The following are major training issues that supervisors will need to face in the electronic library:

1. Quality training will be even more critical.
2. New work patterns and new work will require new training approaches within the context of accelerated change.
3. Training will have to accommodate both the traditional and automated environments.
4. An increasingly diverse staff will require greater flexibility and imagination in training.

5. Training must include more than skills training for staff to be effective in the automated environment.
6. To increase training efficiency, new techniques and approaches to training will be required, and far more training may be centralized in the automated environment.

While training in the traditional library setting is critical to the vitality of the library, it takes on a new dimension as automation is phased into every function and activity. As Mason has stated, "Technology is bringing about an order of magnitude of change. To put it bluntly, the stakes are higher, much higher."[2] Information has become a valued commodity, and there will be an increase in the number and variety of organizations that wish to be the information providers. There are numerous commercial vendors providing access to a variety of databases, and they will increase in the future. On university campuses, the computer center is expanding and may be competing with library services in providing access to online systems. Libraries are going to have to be far more competitive; they will have to be on the "cutting edge" of technology in order to maintain a central role in the information society. This goal cannot be achieved without skilled and knowledgeable staff. Librarians who are comfortable with last year's technology and who are not current and innovative in the use of technology will quickly fall behind, and with them will fall the library.

This means that the commitment to training must improve. Training cannot take a back seat to the multitude of other demands placed on the time and energy of supervisors. As jobs are defined for supervisors and staff, training should be identified as a component of the duties and tasks for which staff will be responsible. Unless there is recognition from this point forward, training will continue to get relegated to the "when we have time" category. In addition, increased funding will be needed to support the quality of training that will be required. Currently, training is usually a hidden cost in libraries; as major automation projects are implemented, funding for training will need to increase in order to support the development of training materials, to provide for trainer positions, and to insure that adequate time is available for staff to learn.

Second, as the work itself changes (e.g., content, patterns, flow, relationships, location), training must shift to relate to the new work. To date, most staff have perceived their work as moving from step to step in a linear fashion until completion, and training has followed this same approach. In the electronic environment, this approach is likely not realis-

2. Marilyn Gell Mason, "The Future of the Public Library," *Library Journal* 110 (Sept. 1, 1985):136.

tic. In some situations, work may be more interactive, such as staff and users communicating online via electronic mail; and in other situations, work may have to be batched, with steps accomplished at different intervals. Training approaches should reflect the differences in work patterns and work flow, as well as develop skills to facilitate the new working relationships that will rely increasingly on interaction via a terminal.

Another major change in work in the automated environment is that the work itself becomes more abstract. Zuboff states that "when information technology reorganizes a job, it fundamentally alters the individual's relation to the task."[3] She refers to this new relationship as "computer-mediated" work. She goes on to say that "with computer-mediated work, employees get feedback about the task object only as symbols through the medium of the information system. Very often, from the point of view of the workers, the object of the task seems to have disappeared 'behind the screen' and into the information system. . . . Computer-mediated work is the electronic manipulation of symbols. Instead of a sensual activity, it is an abstract one." A result of the abstract nature of automated work is that staff can become distant from the objective of their work, lose sight of the importance of the work they perform, and become too focused on technical skills and output. The training process will have to address this potential liability. The movement to a highly automated work environment may be accompanied by a sense of loss of control over the work, because physically the work will be in the system, not in a stack of papers or cards on the desk.

In addition, the language or protocol of a system is very specific, and staff may feel limited because they have no flexibility with the system. Staff have to adapt to the system, and this can lead to frustration and a feeling of loss of creativity in accomplishing work. Staff also have to adapt to time when the system is slow or down. Preparation should be built into training so that staff are able to handle the normal disruptions that occur in an online system. Supervisors should think about what staff might do to remain productive during slow times and should prepare staff emotionally to handle occasional system sluggishness or even a "crash."

As change continues at an accelerated pace, the response time available to plan and implement training will be shorter. In the past, change may have been introduced in a more leisurely fashion, and thus the process of adaptation and training was accomplished over a longer time period. The future does not offer this luxury. Training and retraining will have to occur more frequently in the electronic library.

3. Shoshana Zuboff, "New Worlds of Computer-Mediated Work," *Harvard Business Review* 60 (Sept.–Oct. 1982):144–45.

Third, training will be complicated by the fact that for the immediate future, supervisors will have to be prepared to train staff for both the traditional and the automated environments. It is likely that a library will be neither one nor the other, but a mixture of environments as integrated systems are implemented function by function and as new activities and services emerge to co-exist with certain traditional services that remain vital to library services. Supervisors will have to be knowledgeable in both the traditional and the automated environments, and be capable of training staff in both.

Fourth, most libraries will require an increasingly diverse staff in order to obtain the range of knowledge and skills needed in the high-tech environment. This need is likely to create, in the future, a more heterogeneous library staff, which, in turn, will require flexibility from supervisors in both training and supervision. It is possible that more staff who lack library experience or a master's degree in library science will be recruited. Thus, supervisors may have to expend more time providing basic information about library operations and services than in the past. At the same time, it is inevitable that some library work will be performed by staff in their own homes, thus creating a library cottage industry. Supervisors will have to develop mechanisms for training and retraining these individuals as well, and for maintaining them as members of the organization even though they physically are not in the library.

In the online library environment, it will be necessary for training to include far more than a focus on learning skills. While this new emphasis should be the case also in the traditional library, it becomes even more imperative in the automated environment. Sokol and Bulyk describe a program for training in an integrated information environment as having three components:

- Sensitization—activities that emotionally prepare prospective users for automation.
- Education—activities that intellectually prepare users for using automated tools and further learning.
- Training—activities that actively prepare users to employ new automated tools proficiently.[4]

The authors suggest that training should involve more than imparting skills; it should also focus on making employees more creative and productive problem solvers.

    4. Ellen W. Sokol and John C. Bulyk, "The Truth about Training," *Journal of Information Systems Management* 2 (Fall 1985):76.

In the electronic library, as staff focus more on the database and on the terminal, it will become more important for training to include the broad picture and for staff to develop an understanding of the relationship of their work to the whole. At the same time, the issue of meeting personal and social needs in a highly automated environment requires attention in order to prevent a sense of alienation from the work and from the organization.

As part of this process, staff attitudes toward the process of change and specifically toward the new technology will need to be recognized and addressed. In the automated setting, psychological factors will be more important than ever because of each individual's reactions to the technology and to the impact it will have on his or her work life. It will be important to determine ways to introduce new technology in a positive way and, whenever possible, to introduce it gradually so that learning is accomplished with minimal unease.

Finally, training in the electronic library will require the exploration of new approaches and techniques and very likely the centralizing of a good deal of job training. It will not make sense if a library fully automates and yet does not use the technology to enhance training. Opportunities for computer-assisted instruction (referred to in chapter 3) will be more readily available. As microcomputers are used more broadly in libraries, programs should be developed to provide interactive learning modules. The development of learning modules using computer technology will be important as a way of familiarizing staff with the technology and of increasing cost efficiency in training by encouraging independent and self-paced learning.

Related to this issue is one that will have far-reaching effects on library training—the need to centralize a great deal of job training for automated systems. Because of the sophistication required for training in the high-tech environment, the need to use the technology to design training modules and materials, and the frequency of training and retraining as modifications to systems or new systems are introduced, it will be likely that more job training will occur in a centralized manner. This centralization might be accomplished in several ways, such as through periodic classes being offered by a trainer from a central office as system changes are announced or as staff turnover dictates; or through trainers from a central office who will provide the basic introduction to and skills training for the online system to department staff on an "as needed basis"; or through certain departments that will assume responsibility for training all staff on specific system functions. For instance, if cataloging is distributed to various branch libraries, the training for cataloging on the system may still be provided by the central cataloging department. The same approach could be used for training staff in the circulation function. In these situations, staff requiring training would spend time in the "training" department before assuming their job duties in the "home" department.

The main point is that the way in which training has been accomplished in the past may not be reasonable in the new environment where all staff will have to follow the same requirements in working on an automated system. Greater efficiency and improved quality might also be achieved if training responsibility were centralized, with adequate resources being developed to support the activity and accountability from the training resource being established for quality.

Whatever the specific arrangement, it is likely that more skills training will occur outside of the department. The supervisor, though, will still have to be concerned with establishing a working relationship with the staff member, setting performance goals and expectations, and insuring that the person understands more than just functional skills. Supervisors will also have to remain involved and concerned with any centrally developed training materials and sessions, and then will have to adapt their own training to fit what is provided in this other setting.

All of these factors suggest that training in the electronic library should be vastly different from what exists today. More will be required and expected; supervisors will have to become more sophisticated in their understanding of the relationship between learning and performance, and will have to devote the time and energy needed to respond to training needs in the electronic library.

Summary

The role of staff in creating a dynamic future for libraries has been emphasized throughout the discussion about job training. The assumption is that without increased care and attention being given to this process, the future will be difficult. In *The Change Masters*, Kantor refers to a Renaissance for corporate America, and she describes this environment as one in which organizations "would be more like 'families' making long-term commitments to the development, health, and prosperity of each of their members, and looking to all of them for productive new ideas."[5] Libraries can move toward their Renaissance with training serving as a major vehicle to support staff in mastering the vast array of challenges that lie ahead.

5. Rosabeth Moss Kantor, *The Change Masters: Innovations and Entrepreneurship in the American Corporation* (New York: Simon & Schuster, 1984), p.370.

Appendix A

JOB TRAINING PLANS

The job training plans included here are intended to assist supervisors as they begin to construct their own plans. The job training plans cover different types of positions and are from a variety of libraries. Because of the length of the training plans, only portions of each are provided, mainly those sections that were felt to suggest a useful structure or approach.

The training plans are grouped by job families that should be standard to all libraries: clerical (including student assistant positions), technical, and professional. It is suggested, though, that the reader review all of the training plans in order to benefit from the different approaches and ideas presented in these examples.

Clerical Positions

STUDENT ASSISTANTS
Documents Center
University of Michigan Library
Ann Arbor, Michigan

Author of Training Plan: Sharon Herald

[This training plan is developed in a modular format and is an example of self-instructional material. The employee would receive only those training plans for responsibilities assigned.]

Below is a list of your job responsibilities as well as a training plan for each. It is your responsibility to organize your time to complete each training plan. They are listed in general priority order. However, the sequence does not have to be strictly followed. If you need to skip one training plan and pick it up later you may. All training plans should be completed within the first three weeks of employment.

Job Responsibility	*Training Plan*	
1. Shelf Reading	How to shelf read	_____
2. File Microfiche	How to file microfiche	_____
3. Process Congressional Publications	How to process Congressional pubs	_____
4. Shelving New Publications	How to shelve new publications	_____

Training Plan: How to Shelve New Publications

Job Responsibility: You will shelve all new issues and titles within one week from the time they are put on your shelves.

Training Time: 4 hours

Job Task	*Training Task*
1. Obtain and sort publications from shelves by superv.'s desk	1. Read written instructions
2. File a new title	1. Read & follow instructions Set A
	2. Review work with superv.
3. File a new issue	1. Read & follow instructions Set B
	2. Review work with superv.
4. File microfiche (other than ASI, IIS, SRI microfiche)	1. Read & follow instructions Set C
	2. Review work with superv.

Instructions for Shelving New Material: These instructions will explain the different types of new materials and how to shelve them. You will find the material on the shelves behind your supervisor's desk. It should be divided into different types of materials, but don't be afraid to question if something is on the wrong shelf. Sometimes mistakes occur.

Page #1

If the material is	Then go to instruction set
new title	A
new issues	B
microfiche	C
serial set	D
Arab World File	E
any other publication	notify supervisor

Page #2

Instruction Set A: How to File a New Title

1. Check shelf lists to make sure it is a new title. (New titles will not have cards in the shelf list.)
2. Type 2 cards—one for title file; one for shelf list.
3. Put cards in box marked "new cards."
4. Place publication on proper shelf.

Page #3

Instruction Set B: How to File a New Issue

If there is	then
a call number	go to Step A
no call number	go to Step B

STEP A

1. Look in shelf list and record new issues on any holdings card you find.
2. Follow any special notes on cards.

If the card reads	then
latest ed. in Documents Center	1. record latest ed. 2. place new ed. on shelf 3. pull old ed. from shelf 4. cross location off call # on old ed. 5. place on "stacks" cart by reference desk
latest edition only	1. pull old ed. & throw away 2. put new ed. on shelf
has no special notes	place publication on shelf

STEP B
Look in dictionary title for card.

If	then
you find a card	go to Step A
you don't find a card	check alternate locations
	1. newsletter drawer
	2. census drawer
	3. supervisor

PART-TIME PAGE
　　Circulation
　　Deer Park Public Library
　　Deer Park, Texas

Author of Training Plan: Linda A. Anderson

Training Period: Six Weeks

The following is a training schedule for part-time pages at the Deer
Park Public Library, a small municipal library where everyone does
everything. As each section of the training is introduced, the new employee receives the appropriate section of the procedures manual explaining the specific policy or task. In addition, the page has a file at the
circulation desk for his or her training materials to reference as needed.
Pages are never left alone at the desk until they have completed the six-
week training period.

I.   *First Week*
　　　Introductory material
　　　Opening and closing responsibilities
　　　Patron complaints
　　　Shelf reading
　　　How to use the public catalog
　　　Shelving
II. *Second Week*
　　　Practice skills learned during first week; ask questions
III. *Third Week*
　　　Patron count
　　　Operation of the telephone
　　　Answering patrons' questions
　　　Handling money from patrons
　　　Matching returning books with the proper cards

Training Objectives

I. After Two Weeks Training is completed, the employee should be:
    Familiar with policies and procedures as outlined.
    Able to shelve all materials in the library.
    Able to shelf read in his or her section.
    Able to use the public catalog.

II. After Four Weeks training is completed, the employee should be able to:
    Match all returned items with the proper book card (slip).
    Collect money for all purposes.
    Answer the phone.
    Handle simple directional questions.

STUDENT ASSISTANT
Interlibrary Loan Office
Pullen Library
Georgia State University
Atlanta, Georgia

Author of Training Plan: Janice Mohlhenrich

Welcome to Interlibrary Loan! As when learning any new job, you are about to be bombarded with new information, concepts, and procedures. Don't Panic! Working together with your supervisor, you will follow a training program designed to help you learn the ropes of your new job. The training program will last approximately one month. The first weeks will focus on providing basic information related to the initial activities that you will be responsible for assuming and will help to familiarize you with the services provided by the Interlibrary Loan Office. You and your supervisor will review your training on a regular basis to assess your progress and smooth out any areas where you may be experiencing difficulty. The training plan is not inclusive—other information identified during the training will be included. Your questions, comments, and suggestions will be welcomed at any time. We're glad to have you here!

Objectives

Familiarize the student assistant with the tools and techniques necessary for the successful completion of tasks listed in the job description.

1) Orient student to the physical location of departments in library;
2) Introduce other students and staff with whom he or she will work;
3) Establish working patterns for most efficient handling of work loads;

4) Set guidelines for behavior; and
5) Outline expectations in regard to amount of work to be completed
   each day.

Working Tools	*Date of Expected Proficiency*	*Met*
OLLI	2 weeks	
COM catalog	2	
card catalog	2	
shelf list	1	
periodical list	1	
circulation print out	1	
opening packages	1	
OCLC terminal	2 months	
files	1	
truck house	1 week	
AAUC microfiche	2	
microform printer	3	
photocopy machine	1	

[A daily training schedule follows.]

Training Plan: Second Week

During the second week of training, you and your supervisor will work together to help you refine the skills and techniques you acquired during the early part of your training. Please question, comment, suggest about procedures—if something seems difficult, perhaps there is a better way, and your comments will help. The objective of your training is to enable you to do your job successfully and efficiently. Each day you will be responsible for completing the following tasks:

1) get call numbers for the requests
2) pull books and periodicals
3) do photocopy
4) open packages

The number of requests received varies from day to day, so it is difficult to predict the length of time required for each of the above tasks. In order to assess an average time for these tasks and as a way for you to assess your own progress, please record the following information daily for the remaining three weeks of your training period:

# of Requests ALA	Amt Time OCLC	Amt Time to get call #	Amt Time pulling books	Remarks photocopy

Sample questions from a questionnaire given to student assistants during their training:

1. Do you feel the training thus far has prepared you to successfully complete assigned tasks?
2. Have you been given enough information? Are explanations adequate?
3. Have your trainers been well-prepared? Knowledgeable? Helpful? Difficult to work with? Confusing?
4. Do you feel comfortable asking questions and are your questions answered satisfactorily?
5. Generally has the training each day been a positive or a negative experience? Why?

SECRETARY
Library Personnel Office
University of Michigan Library
Ann Arbor, Michigan

Author of Training Plan: Lucy Cohen

The training for the secretary position will cover approximately 4 to 6 months. The first 2 to 4 weeks will focus on providing basic information on the initial activities that the incumbent is responsible for and to provide an introduction to the services of the Library Personnel Office.

This plan outlines the areas of information that should be covered. It is not expected to be inclusive, and other information will be added as identified.

The incumbent will meet with the supervisor on a weekly basis for review during the first four weeks. These meetings will allow for a review of the secretary's progress and any problems with the training, as well as identifying any area(s) that need further attention or clarification.

Recruitment and Hiring of Regular Support Staff

During the first two weeks, the secretary will be trained to assume responsibility for all the routines involved in this function including:

preparing, distributing, and posting vacancy announcements,
scheduling interviews, and typing tests as requested,
providing reference checks as requested,
preparing appointment activity records,
making the job offer,
scheduling orientation with University Personnel.

Eventually as the secretary becomes more knowledgeable about the University's affirmative action and employment policies as well as special needs in the Library, she will be able to assist supervisors in all facets of recruitment and hiring of regular support staff, including:

- Provide information about preparation of job descriptions and selection criteria,
- Assist in determining if affirmative action, reduction-in-force, and promotional opportunities program policies have been adhered to,
- Assist in determining if fair employment practices have been met.

Once the routines for support of employment activities for regular support staff are learned, the secretary will assume responsibility for support of Librarian employment activities as well.

Files, Records

During the first two weeks, the secretary will be trained to maintain personnel office files. As she becomes familiar with the files and related procedures, she will be responsible for organizing and weeding of files.

The secretary will be supported to attend the University's training session on organization of files.

Personal Contacts

Contact with staff and visitors to the Library Personnel Office is a primary role in this position. It is the goal of the Library Personnel Office to offer accurate and timely information in a pleasant and courteous manner. Training for this will involve:

learning to answer the phone in a pleasant and courteous manner and taking appropriate messages,
becoming familiar with Library organization and staff,
being familiar with the typical questions asked of the LPO,
being familiar with forms and other materials requested by staff and/or applicants.

Technical Positions

LIBRARY ASSISTANT
Acquisition Department
Texas Tech University
Lubbock, Texas

Author of Training Plan: Carol Kelley

Training Objective. To have the new employee learn all library procedures necessary to perform duties required for this position.

Content. Work involves order and payment of subscriptions, single issues, and back runs. Orders are placed with both domestic and foreign vendors. This work requires the ability to learn invoice processing, machine readable and manual serial holding files, use of OCLC terminals, filing, and other related tasks. This position requires judgment, and the ability to cope with varying work flow patterns.

Sequence of Training and Time Allowed to Learn Tasks

1st Week: 1. Tour of Library
Time Allowed: 1 hour
2. Explanation of procedure manual
Time Allowed: 1 1/2 hours
3. Explanation of how subscription interacts with the serials work flow
Time Allowed: 1 hour
4. Sorting 1st Class mail & checking invoices
Time Allowed: 1 week
5. Processing of invoices & accounting procedures
Time Allowed: 2 weeks
6. Correspondence & Filing
Time Allowed: 1 month
7. Responding to payment problems
Time Allowed: 1 month

Although we have gone through the training procedures in only two weeks, we do not expect this person to be fully trained without continued supervision. Within 3 months items 1–5, 8, 11 should be totally understood and carried through without supervision. Within 6 months items 6, 7, 9, 10 should be understood and carried through without supervision unless a problem is unusual and cannot be solved with the usual steps learned in training.

LIBRARY TECHNICAL ASSISTANT
Serials Unit
Pullen Library
Georgia State University
Atlanta, Georgia

Author of Training Plan: Judith Shelton

Introduction: The objectives of this plan are to train you in the skills and knowledge required to catalog serials independently in accordance with standards and local requirements.

This plan is not intended to be rigid nor to include everything. The time frames suggested may be adjusted depending on your pace in learning or the quantity and kind of materials received for cataloging. Components may be rescheduled or rearranged, and additional topics may be introduced as the need for them is identified during the process of training.

Training Feedback, and Evaluation. Approximately the first nine months or so will be a period of intensive training, followed by a period of some three months or so of increasing independence in straightforward cataloging along with continued instruction in original and member library cataloging and in various serial cataloging processes.

It is expected that by the end of the first year you will be working fairly independently, and that you will be able to meet the quantitative norms defined in the Minimum Output Standards for Serials Catalogers. Our expectations for paraprofessionals in the Serials Unit are outlined in detail in the departmental administrative manual.

Primary responsibility for training and evaluation will rest with the supervisor, but there will be occasions when other staff will be involved in the training process. We will meet frequently at first, and at least weekly during the first six to nine months. You are encouraged to submit your work with notes on questions, uncertainties, your interpretation of the cataloging rules, etc. You may always propose additional discussion sessions beyond what we schedule. Besides the informal meetings mentioned above, there will be formal evaluations held after two months, at the end of the first six months, and at six-month intervals thereafter.

[An explanation of the revision process followed.]

Training Schedule:

I. General Orientation
   A. Read Library Administrative Manual
   B. Read Catalog Department Administrative Manual
   C. Read Serials Cataloging Manual, Section 1
   D. Read Periodicals Cataloging Manual, Section 1
   E. Read Osburn's Serial Publications, p. 3–19, 193–228
   F. Read Wynar's *Introduction to Cataloging & Classification*, p. 184–185
II. Progression of Cataloging Assignments
   A. Shelf list revision

1. Read GCM, Section 28
2. Read PM, Section 11
B. Periodical added volumes which do not need updates
1. Read GCM, Section 16, 21, 49
2. Read PM, Section 4, 6, 7, 12

Requirements for Paraprofessionals in the Serials Unit

By the end of the first three months of work:
Be able to catalog with a minimum of difficulty periodical and serial added volumes which involve no cataloging changes and to recognize changes of entry.
Be able to revise satisfactorily the periodicals shelf list.
By the end of the first six months of work:
Be able to catalog without revision and at the minimum rate of speed periodical added volumes which involve no cataloging changes.
Be able to catalog satisfactorily and at the minimum rate of speed monographic and serial added volumes and to recognize cataloging problems and irregularities that come to light when volumes are added.
Be able to revise satisfactorily the serials shelf list.
[Continues through first year. Also included are quantity and minimum output standards.]

REFERENCE DESK ASSISTANT
Graduate Reference Department
University of Michigan Library
Ann Arbor, Michigan

Author of Training Plan: Kathy Tezla

This training plan will be used to guide your orientation in the Graduate Library Reference Department. The orientation will consist of lectures, reading assignments, exercises, observations, and practice. All members of the Department will participate in the training program.

At the end of each week, you will meet with the Head of the Reference Department to discuss your progress and observations of the training program.

The training program is designed to provide continuous feedback on your performance. At the end of the first month, the Head of Reference will provide an informal review of your progress in advance of the formal probationary review.

The objectives of the training plan are:

1. To develop a knowledge of the bibliographic record, the public card catalog, and the online bibliographic search system.
2. To develop a knowledge of information sources.
3. To develop basic public service communication skills for reference service, such as reference interviewing, search strategies, problem patrons.
4. To develop an understanding of the role of the Technical Library Assistant in the philosophy and practice of reference service.

Initial Discussion of Service Desk Skills

Objective: To provide a general introduction to attitudes and skills necessary for effective public service desk work.
Contents/Sequence:
    Basic Reference Interviewing Concepts
    Attitudes Toward User
        Courtesy
        Professionalism
        Problem Patrons
    Teaching Function of public services staff
Length of Time: 1½ hours for presentation/discussion.
1 to 2 hours for trainee to read articles.
Suggested Materials:
    Reference Interview:
        Bunge, Charles A., "Interpersonal Dimensions of the Reference Interview: A Historical Review of the Literature," *Drexel Library Quarterly* 20, p. 4–23.
        "The Reference Interview" in Davinson, D. E., and Bingley, C., *Reference Services*. London: Clive Bingley, 1980, p. 77–92.
    Problem Patrons:
        Vocino, Michael, "The Library and the Problem Patron," *Wilson Library Bulletin* (January 1976), p. 372–73.

Reference Desk II: Reference Interview
Objectives: To assist in developing a question negotiation ability that is able to define and encourage inquiry for reference service.
Contents/Sequence: Using specific selections from the literature that are read prior to the session(s), discuss the following:
    definition of the reference interview
    the reference process (definition, components)
    reference interview style (personality of person at desk, nonverbal communication)
    reference techniques ("step interview")
Length of Time: 4 hours for each section
Suggested Materials: [Specific articles are provided.]

Reference Desk III: Telephone Service
Objective: To explain the philosophy, mechanics, and etiquette of telephone reference service.
Contents/Sequence:
Outline the philosophy of telephone reference service: differences & similarities with in-person reference work.
Explain the mechanics of telephone service: putting someone on hold, transferring a call, use of local extension, etc.
Describe good telephone etiquette: how to answer, the appropriate length of time to leave someone on hold, returning a call, etc.
Length of Time: 30 minutes

Public Card Catalog I: Introduction
Objective: To serve as a general introduction to the Graduate Library Public Card Catalog outlining its special characteristics, in addition to providing instruction in the basic knowledge of the Catalog Card and the Computer Card formats.
Contents/Sequence:
Catalog Card
Catalog Card Set (main entry, subject, added entries)
References
Practice Exercise
Pre-AACR2/AACR2 Computer-Produced Card Format
Practice Exercise
Union Catalog Concept
How to Determine Locations in Public Card Catalog
Length of Time: 2 hours with a 15-minute break
Suggested Materials:
Oversize visual aids of catalog card
Transparencies of samples from Michigan card catalog

Public Card Catalog II: Filing Rules
Objective: To bring into focus the arrangement of entries in the public card catalog describing the concept of a dictionary catalog and the basic filing rules on which to build on one's understanding of the catalog arrangement.
Contents/Sequence:
Definition of Dictionary Catalog
Publications Not Included in Public Catalog
Publications Only Partially Represented
General Rules for Filing:
Author:
Length of Time: 2 half-days with time for review
Suggested Materials:
Shakespeare drawer
Michigan drawer

U.S. government drawer
Filing Rules Handout

[This training plan has many more components relating to the reference tasks and reference sources. In addition, a specific training schedule has been developed for the first 25 days of training.]

Professional Positions

MONOGRAPH CATALOGER
  Processing Division/Original Cataloging Department
  Sterling C. Evans Library
  Texas A&M University
  College Station, Texas

Author of Training Plan: Christine E. Thompson

Training Objectives: To train entry-level monographic catalogers:
  to search for appropriate cooperative cataloging copy on OCLC,
  to describe a monograph according to AACR2 standards,
  to assign LC subject headings and call numbers to the described ma-
    terials,
  to prepare OCLC work forms for input by the terminal processors
    in the Copy Cataloging Department.

Length of Training:
  1st quarter: departmental background, LCSH, and call number as-
    signment familiarization
  2nd quarter: original cataloging, including AACR2 descriptive,
    OCLC search techniques
  3rd quarter: OCLC searching and input editing
  4th quarter: sharpening skills obtained in the first three quarters.

Schedule

Time Period: 1st Month
Trainer:
Objectives: To become familiar with processing procedures and poli-
  cies relative to the operation of the Original Cataloging Depart-
  ment.
Departmental Overview:
Scheduled Meetings: [Completed in Plan]
Specific Tasks:
Background Readings:
Attachments:

Time Period: 2nd Month
Trainer:
Objectives: To become familiar with:
    the technique of subject analysis
    the use of the LC Subject Headings list
    the use of the LC classification schedules for call number assign-
        ment.
Training Overview:
    The month will be spent in one-on-one training sessions with the
trainer, learning the necessary skills for adequate subject analysis and
assignment of classification numbers.
Scheduled Meetings:
    Weekly meetings for the first two weeks with the Head of Original
Cataloging Department and the trainer for updating and planning.
Specific Tasks:
    Become familiar with handling cooperative cataloging copy refer-
rals from Copy Cataloging Department.
    Become familiar with the LC Subject Headings list and manual, as
well as explanatory texts used by the department.
    Become familiar with using the LC classification schedules, as well
as explanatory texts used by the department.
Background Readings:
    Procedures manuals
    Cataloger's Bookshelf

[Training Plan has similar outline through 12 months.]

SELECTORS
    Alfred Taubman Medical Library
    University of Michigan
    Ann Arbor, Michigan

Author of Training Plan: Dottie Eakin

Objectives: When training has been completed, the selector should:

1. Be familiar with basic principles of collection development.
2. Know the general structure of the UM programs in each field of
   selection responsibility: instructional programs, research emphasis, clinical services.
3. Be broadly familiar with current emphasis and major issues or con-
   troversies in research, diagnosis, or treatment. Know who the leaders in the field are.
4. Be able to identify the major professional organizations in the field.
5. Know the key journals in the field, the best sources for book reviews, and the primary texts and review publications.

6. Understand current collecting criteria for the Taubman Medical Library and be able to apply them to selection of new books in the field.
7. Understand and be able to carry out selection responsibilities.

Training Plan

It is expected that each section would be covered in one week, including preparation time and a one to two hour session for discussion. Sections 4 to 6 would be repeated for each major subject field to be covered.

Section 1: Principles of Collection Development
Preparation/Reading:
> *Handbook of Medical Library Practice*, 4th ed., Chapter 2.
> ALA *Guidelines for Collection Development*, p.1–30.
> Collection Policy Statements for UM libraries.
> Description of the RLG cooperative collection management program and conspectus.

Discussion:
> Factors affecting collection development
> Types of selection criteria
> Policy development
> Levels of collecting
> History of Taubman collections.

Section 2: Organization for Selection at Taubman
Preparation/Reading:
> Distribution of subjects among selectors
> Description of Serials Review Committee responsibilities and procedures.

Discussion:
> Responsibilities of selectors
> Sources of information about books
> Procedures; time expectations
> Departmental consultants
> Serials Review Committee
> Reference materials
> Budget: allocation and monitoring of funds
> Technical processing functions (Taubman Medical)
> Technical services functions (Graduate Library)

Section 3: Selection Criteria
Preparation/Reading:
> Taubman Medical Library Collection Policy
> Guidelines for selection at Taubman
> Lists of review journals for subject areas

Talk with current selector about sources, areas of importance, problem areas, method of keeping up with review journals.

Discussion:

Criteria for selection

Application of criteria

Review of sample ads, approval forms, book reviews, and selection decisions

Plan preparation for next session.

[Format continues through four other topics.]

REFERENCE LIBRARIANS
General Reference Division
Dallas Public Library
Dallas, Texas

Author of Training Plan: Miriam Martin

[Material taken from a training manual that includes pre- and post-test materials as well as a training plan.]

Objectives:

To know the basic functions of the library's computer terminal,

To know the arrangements and uses of basic (general) reference sources,

To know the functions, duties, and responsibilities of the Information and General Reference Service Desks,

To be knowledgeable of all policies, procedures, and publications of the Dallas Public Library system and guidelines for specific reference requests,

To better understand the Library's philosophy of public and reference services.

WEEK I [portion]

Responsibility: Reference Sources/Part I

Task: Learn the arrangement and use of basic reference sources
Dictionaries, encyclopedias, almanacs, handbooks, directories, indexes, etc.
Learn how to use microforms

Trainer:

Materials:

Reference Training Manual

AHE List, Dun & Bradstreet List

Training Task Completed (indicate):

WEEK II [portion]
Responsibility: Reference Sources/Part II
Task: Learn the arrangement and use of subject sources
        Learn how to use *Reader's Guide to Periodical Literature*
Trainer:
Materials: *Readers' Guide to Periodical Literature*
Training Task Completed (indicate):

WEEK III [portion]
Responsibility: 24-Hour Reference Services
Task: Learn how to operate the telephone answering machine
        Learn how to record questions/answers from machine
        Learn how to change daily tapes, etc.
Trainer:
Materials: 24-Hour Machine and Manual
Training Task Completed (indicate):

WEEK IV–VI [portion]
Responsibility: Reference Sources/Part III
Task: Learn how to use *Facts on File* and *Standard Rate and Data*
        Pre-test will be given on basic reference sources
Trainer:
Materials: *Facts on File*
Training Task Completed:

WEEKS VII–VIII [portion]
Responsibility: Reference Post-test
Task: Post-test will include all materials and services discussed
Trainer:
Materials: Post-test

MANAGER, LIBRARY PERSONNEL/PAYROLL OFFICE
    University of Michigan Library
    Ann Arbor, Michigan

Author of Training Plan: Sheila Creth

The formal training for this position will cover approximately six to
eight months. The initial four to six weeks will focus on providing basic
information for those activities that the incumbent will assume initially
and provide an introduction to University and Library personnel policies and procedures. This plan outlines the areas of information that
should be covered. It is not expected to be inclusive, and other infor-
mation/topics will be added as they are identified. While the training
schedule may have to be shifted in order to accommodate situations in
the Office, the integrity of the training plan should be maintained.

The incumbent will meet with her supervisor weekly over the first eight weeks in order to provide a review of progress, address any problems with the training, and identify issues that need to be clarified.

Recruitment (Week 1 & 2)

Materials: Articles on Recruitment
    University & Library Policy/Procedures
    University & Library Forms
Discussion of following with Supervisor:
    purpose and philosophy of recruitment
    normal turnover patterns in Library
    status of current vacancies
    identification of policies, procedures, and existing problems for all
      job families (clerical, P & A, librarians, student assistants)
    search strategies for professional positions
    identification of specific priorities and timetable for addressing recruitment issues/problems.
Discussion of following with University Employment Office:
    University policies and procedures for clerical and P & A recruitment
    Paperwork and timetable for forwarding materials
    Clarification of services provided by central Employment Office.

In addition, meet with clerical staff that handle recruitment and discuss their activities and work flow, observe the process.

During this period, complete the paperwork for at least one search in each job family (if available).

Also, review the following in order to develop a familiarity with how professional positions are advertised: *Chronicle of Higher Education, American Libraries, College & Research Libraries, Library Journal.*

Review search files currently vacant and previous ones in order to grasp the process and information required.

Attend the University offered workshop on "Hiring Process and Selection Interviewing."

By the end of the first three weeks, the Manager should have gained an overview of the work flow, procedures, and policies related to recruitment for all job family groups.

There will still be questions, particularly for professional recruitment, and these will be discussed as the training progresses.

In addition, by the end of the three weeks, the Manager should have identified certain aspects of the recruitment program which require attention—specifically for the temporary/student assistant and clerical recruitment.

It is expected that within six months, the Manager will have a solid grasp of recruitment practices and be operating independently regarding all routine searches.

[The training plan covers other personnel functions.] The goal of the training program is to have the Manager assume the full range of responsibilities outlined in the job description within six to eight months. It is anticipated, though, that the incumbent will still require general assistance and direction over the next year to two years as she develops an expertise in personnel administration.

Appendix B

ORIENTATION CHECKLIST

Employee Name _____

Department/Unit _____ Position _____

[This checklist *can be* used by the supervisor to ensure that all working conditions have been explained to the new employee. Other items could be added to suit local needs.]

A. *The Job*
____ position description
____ training plan/schedule
____ department goals
____ department organization chart
____ department staff names & position titles
____ library organization chart
____ list library staff/phone numbers
____ other

B. *Physical Surroundings*
Introduction to:
____ co-workers
____ work area
____ equipment/supplies
____ restrooms
____ bulletin boards

____ staff lounge
____ eating facilities
____ parking arrangements

C. *Hours of Work*
____ work week & schedule
____ flexible scheduling
____ meals/rest periods
____ calling in sick, etc.
____ medical appointments, etc.
____ release-time classes, workshops, etc.

D. *Leave*
____ vacation
____ sick
____ holidays
____ leaves without pay
____ other

117

E.   *Compensation*
____ pay rate
____ when paid
____ where paid
____ raises
____ overtime
____ comp time

F.   *Evaluation*
____ annual
____ salary
____ merit

G.   *Benefits*
____ tuition
____ medical
____ retirement
____ other

H.   *Rights/Responsibilities*
____ attendance
____ punctuality
____ safety
____ other

INDEX

Prepared by Gene Heller

Ability: defined, 3; job analysis and, 30
Adult learning environment, 15–16
Anxiety, new employee and, 18
Attitude of trainee, 3–4, newly hired, 17–20; supervisor's effect on, 11
Automation: electronic library and, 94–96; increased use of, 2; resistance to change and, 6, 7; training materials and, 71

Case study method of training, 48
Centralization of training, electronic library and, 95–96
Change agent, 5–6
Closed-minded trainers, 64–65
Co-worker assistance for trainee, 64
Coaching, 86
Communication during training, 58–66; conflicting messages and, 63–64; co-worker trainee assistance and, 64; criticism and, 62, 63; jargon and, 65–66; learning difficulty and, 61–62; mistakes by trainee and, 63–64; pace of training and, 61; praise and, 60, 62; trainee feedback and, 58–61; training style and, 61–66. *See also* Questioning
Computer-assisted instruction, 47, 95–96
Computer-mediated work, 92–93
Conferences, training opportunities of, 90–91
Conflicting messages from trainer, 63–64
Corporate culture, 4; supervisor's effect on, 6
Costs of training: benefits vs., 10–11; evaluation of, 75, 78–79

Critical tasks: job analysis and, 29; order of presentation of, 39–41
Criticism, communication and, 62, 63

Demonstration method of training, 44
Department needs and training schedule, 71
Discussion method of training, 45–46
Dissatisfiers, motivation and, 55–56

Electronic library, 91–96
Evaluation of training, 73–84; appropriate times for, 79–83; costs and, 10, 76, 78–79; goals of, 73–74; objectives in, 76–77; responsibility for, 75; review meetings and, 80–81; supervisory role in, 81, 83; trainee performance and, 76–77; utility of, 83
Experienced employees, performance problems of, 19–22

False assumptions about training, 12–13
Feedback from trainee, 58–61
Functional job requirements, 28

Glossary, jargon and, 65–66
Goal setting, 87–88

Hierarchy of needs, 54–55
Hygiene factors, motivation and, 56

Instructional materials, 68–69

Jargon, 65–66
Job analysis, 27–32
Job descriptions, 28

Job requirements, 28–32
Job security: motivation and, 57;
    operational changes and, 24

"Knowledge work," 85; performance
    standards and, 34
Knowledge: defined, 3; job analysis and,
    29–30

Learning difficulty, communication and,
    61–62
Learning environment, 15–16; evaluation of
    training and, 77; positive feelings and,
    18–19
Learning principles, 14–15
Lecture method of training, 45
Library committees, training opportunities
    of, 88

Management approaches, inadequate
    training and, 10
Manuals, 69
Materials, 67–70; instructional, 68–69;
    orientation, 67; training cost and, 79
Meetings, training opportunities of, 88–89
Methods of training, 43–49; case study, 48;
    demonstration, 44–45; discussion, 45;
    lecture, 45; programmed instruction,
    46–47; role play, 47–48; selection of,
    48–49
Mistakes by trainee, communication and,
    63–64
Motivation, 53–57; hierarchy of needs and,
    54; job security and, 57;
    motivator-hygiene concept and, 55–56;
    training environment and, 57
Motivator-hygiene concept, 55–56
Multiple trainees: operational problems
    and, 22–25; training schedule and, 72

Newly hired trainees, 11, 17–20; previous
    experience of, 19

Objectives for trainee, performance
    standards and, 36–38
OCLC, job security and, 24–25
One-on-one training, 44
Operational changes and problems, 22–25
Orientational materials, 67–68

Pace of training, 61
Performance goals, 87–88
Performance problems, 20–22; analysis of,
    21–22
Performance standards, 32–36; evaluation of
    training and, 76–77; "knowledge

work" and, 34, 85; results of
    orientation of, 33–34
Planning for training, 26–52; flexibility in,
    51; job analysis and, 27–32; methods of
    training and, 43–49; order of
    presentation and, 39–41; performance
    standards and, 32–36; trainer selection
    and, 41–43; training objectives and,
    36–39; written plan and, 49–52
Praise, communication and, 62, 63
Pre-training evaluation, 79–80
Presentation order of training information,
    39–41
Programmed instruction, 46–47

Questioning by trainee, 13; closed-minded
    trainers and, 64–65; newly hired, 18.
    See also Communication

Reference desk, training evaluation and,
    81–82
Reference librarian, 6; training sequence
    for, 40
Resistance to change, 7; operational changes
    and, 24
Retraining experienced employees, 19–22
Review meetings: communication and,
    58–59; evaluation of training and,
    80–81
Role modeling, 86–87
Role play method of training, 47–48

Satisfiers, motivation and, 55–56
Scheduling training, 70–71
Sequence of training, planning and, 39–41
Skill: defined, 3; job analysis and, 29–30
Socialization, 4–5
Staff diversity, electronic library and, 93–95
Staff resistance to change, 7
Structured discussion, 45–46
Supervisor effectiveness, 9
Supervisor's false assumptions, 12–14
Supervisory coaching, 86

Teaching function of supervisors, 11
Technology, increased use of, 2. See also
    Automation
Terminology, 65–66
Time allocated for tasks, job analysis and,
    29
Trainer: characteristics of, 42–43;
    conflicting messages from, 63–64;
    evaluation of training and, 78, 80–81;
    selection of, planning and, 41–43
Training environment, motivation and, 57

Training objectives, performance standards and, 36–39
Training plan. *See* Planning for training
Training process and trainee attitude, 3–4; evaluation of training and, 77
Training style, communication and, 61–65

Understaffing, 10
Unstructured discussion, 45, 46
User, changing needs of, 2

Workshops, training opportunities of, 89–90
Writing training plans, 50–52

Sheila D. Creth is the Assistant Director for Administrative Services at the University of Michigan Library at Ann Arbor. For over ten years she has developed and led training programs on management and organization topics for libraries and library associations. She has written articles for *Library Journal, Drexel Library Quarterly,* and the *Journal of Academic Librarianship.*